THE
SENSIBLE LIFE

THE
SENSIBLE LIFE

The Reflections of a Psychiatrist
Life is an interpretation but not an illusion.

. . .

Robert D. Martin, M.D.

ISBN: 1517431824
ISBN 13: 9781517431822

I would like to dedicate this book to my family, and, especially, to my grandchildren, Zaylee and Aria. I hope someday they will read this book and feel a connection with their grandfather while obtaining some small benefit from its text.

CONTENTS

PREFACE

• • •

AFTER PRACTICING PSYCHIATRY FOR NEARLY fifty years, I feel a need to share some of my insights. I am now seventy-six. If I had thought that I would live another fifty years, I probably would not have written this book. Wisdom is never complete. I can't imagine what my opinions would be fifty years from now. I would hope they would be the same as those you have before you in this work, but uncertainty prevails.

Although my book encompasses a variety of ideas regarding language, the relationship between the brain and the body, and the nature of scientific inquiry, much of what I say can be summarized in a few simple statements. Language is the trap we live in; any attempt to understand the world is contaminated by it. Truth is an asymptote, a conclusion attempted and never reached; however, what we hold as true must be repeatedly tested by scientific scrutiny. Truth is analogous to the curve on a graph where the curved line approaches the intersecting end but never reaches it. We are our brains. The mind-body dilemma, or the erroneous belief the mind is separate from the brain, is a fantasy perpetuated by language. The mind and the brain are one, a fact easily said but difficult to prove. We are far from connecting brain biology (neurons, glia, synapses, protein formation in memory, and ionic transportations into and out of cells) to the fact that the mind is created by the brain. It is important that we not mystify this process by our ignorance, but it is also important not to presume we know more than we do.

The book begins with the psychology of relationships. This is not a theoretical edifice designed to construct an all-encompassing truth about people; rather, I attempt to emphasize elements often overlooked when examining why people act the way they do toward each other. The most important idea here is that the individual tends to see the world with self-reference. He or she has a devil of a time looking at what's really happening between him- or herself and the other person. This narcissistic perspective derives from childhood and is an example of a lack of full maturity. In maturity we realize that in dyadic experiences, there are two feeling and thinking people involved. The other person's behavior is an indication of who that person is and how he or she feels; it is not an indication of the worth of the person to whom the behavior is applied. I cannot emphasize enough how often this basic idea is missed in relationships.

In this book, I am attempting to express principles that help us to work our way through life in a meaningful and rational way. This means that while giving emotions their due, these feelings have to be kept in check and simultaneously allowed to temper reasoning. You cannot isolate emotions from cognition, nor should you. Both are indicators and managers of daily experience. The sensible life knows this and incorporates it into all considerations.

You cannot benefit from the ideas offered here if you're impoverished and threatened. All of these thoughts are for people with food on the table, enough money to feel comfortable in fulfilling daily needs, and an environment that is free of war. If the Taliban is at the door, there is no sensible life. Your job at that moment is to flee. We cannot expect the continually endangered to benefit from wisdom that does not deal with the danger of the moment. This book is not an "adjustment to war" manual; it teaches us how to live in peaceful times.

This is also not a book designed to help those with severe social instability. A survival manual is what you need when Mom is on crack and Dad has abandoned you. The ideas here are for those who did not have that degree of pain and torment. Dealing with posttraumatic stress disorder from childhood is distinct from adjusting to a troubled boss or understanding a serious relationship gone awry. Though I do have a great deal to say about the abused child once he or she has grown into an adult, I have mostly left that material out of this book. Frankly, it is quite difficult to make wise comments about what to do with an addicted mother, an irresponsible father, or a house filled with physical abuse. A child can't flee. Foster homes are not usually much of an improvement. It's a terrible situation. I often observed this circumstance with feelings of helplessness, knowing my meager interventions would make little difference. Although the resilience of human beings is always impressive, and a ghetto child might bounce back from the scars of an abusive and chaotic home life, no one goes away from this without scars. In these histories, major social changes on a societal level are often the only solutions.

This book is made up of ideas that are not original. Any one of them can be found in contemporary literature. However, in the aggregate, I believe I have something to offer. My main theme is that we live in uncertainty. Language, like gravity, gives us a false sense of direction and a false sense of confidence. The mystery of it all is greater than the explanation. We would all be better off to accept this. The answer is not nihilism, but a kind of constructionism. We need to construct a consistent framework for society to work. Religion is useful if everyone universally agrees with its principles. Since this is highly unlikely, it should be replaced by a general concordance that humanity deserves safety and comfort. All people should behave in a manner consistent with that end. If religion is defined as a belief system based on consistent reasoning designed to improve the well-being of humanity, one may argue that my constructed framework is a religion in and of itself. However, religion as we usually experience it in its institutional forms usually breeds conflict. Everyone holds to his or her beliefs as a badge of superiority toward others. This is religion with a capital *R* and has no place in this book.

There is no philosophy that can please all, and it is likely humankind will battle with itself in the near future. Certainly, I am no utopian. I would not even want to be. There is no utopia. I do think that humanity, if it becomes aware of the mystery of existence, will be a humbler and less combative humanity than the one we have now. Currently, there are factions in human society that believe they have the only answer; worse, these people want to convince through force that others should submit to that answer. These groups do not acknowledge any of the thoughts promulgated in this text. They are overconfident, believe in their language (whatever it might be), and are determined to dominate. Many of those who make up the population of these aggressive people come from troubled and abusive homes. This contributes to but does not change the fact that they have not opened their eyes to what the world is really about.

I have been repeatedly impressed with how suffering patients have a constricted view of interpersonal relationships and the way the world actually operates. The distortions of understanding others and their limited worldviews are handicaps in their ability to adapt. Helping someone see that a relative is not hurtful because he or she has a clear wish to hurt, but hurtful because he or she is troubled and confused is often the rewarding moment in many therapeutic experiences. This and learning to live with uncertainty are the mainstays of therapy. They rest side by side with the need to explore and appreciate the family historical influences on how they feel and see the world.

Ironically, most of the world's population wants to live peaceably, rear their children, and have good psychological relationships. If this were not the case, the human part of our planet would never have developed to its current remarkable state. Those who make up this live-and-let-live perspective are responsible for keeping the always-present human pathology in check.

My hope is that some of the ideas in *The Sensible Life* will help in this endeavor.

INTRODUCTION

• • •

LIFE HAS NEVER BEEN EASY. We entered into the world extruded from narrow canals, our skulls squeezed, our bodies contorted to make the passage. This emergence happens with the painful sounds of our mothers' exertions, the administrations of others, and the clipping of the one tie that connects us to our mothers' bodies. Once outside of the protective environment of our mothers' buoyant fluids, we are slapped with the affectionate encouragement to cry our existence into being. We would protest if we knew the truth of what was transpiring. Deaf to our vocal contentions, our caretakers forcibly release us from the biological mooring of motherhood. We begin the adjustment to our new temporal home consisting of parents, town, state, country, planet, galaxy, and universe.

During our gestation we were protected, knowing only, as amoeboid organisms know, the fluids surrounding us, but not knowing in the sense that *Homo sapiens sapiens* know. The challenge for *Homo sapiens sapiens* comes with the rest of life. "Knowing" becomes a complex and progressive undertaking, gathering information and understanding as the years pass. This not only depends on hearing, touching, feeling, and seeing, but, most importantly, on language. Born in Japan, the United States, or Mongolia, we learn the language of our place from the words spoken by our parents. Our DNA encoded in our body cells gives the learning potential to our brains; these genes are fixed from conception. The language is oddly parochial, settled in the house, the town, and the region of our development. Thus begins the nature-nurture question: How much is genetic, and how much is environment? Language strongly indicates the two are intertwined and crucial. No matter how much the DNA in us may set up the nerves of the brain to understand a language, if the language isn't there, no vocabulary is acquired, no nouns or verbs are used, and the foundation of being a human being is not established.

The infant newly emerged is not a tabula rasa, not an empty slate for the imprints of civilization to be made, but a potential person. The genes are in place for that person to emerge. Yet, if the emergence is not in a hospitable environment that slowly nurtures, he or she becomes a limited being, someone with, perhaps, severe problems.

Aside from language, there is another crucial nature-nurture issue. Morality is created, not given. Despite the fervent teachings of the Catholic Church, a child is not born as a sinner. A child is born ignorant, largely a biological specimen, and divorced of any sense of right or wrong. Like language, which is a necessary constituent of moral learning, morality is developed, not inherent. Right and wrong are very much social constructs, but the ability of a child to understand these values is genetic. Available evidence asserts that certain lesions in the brain may result in the sense of right or wrong (as society defines them in a specific culture) being lost. You need the frontal lobe—even special areas in the frontal lobe—to appreciate moral values. Language is similar. You need special areas known to process language to learn and use language. Try as they might, many a poor stroke victim has lost the ability to articulate known words and ideas.

Both language and morality are developed. The nascent adult child understands little of his or her own value and less of how others figure in the scheme of things. Whether matters such as ownership or fairness are inherent in children's thinking may be debated and researched, but there is little question that the presence of social values is largely learned. This is an especially important idea when it comes to how adults view themselves. An abused child likely grows up to feel second rate, not good enough, as if something is wrong. They see the world as inimical or threatening. These children have learned that their value is dubious; their parents were not supportive and encouraging, and, therefore, they provided no secure foundation. This conviction becomes so strong that it becomes difficult for a therapist to help the patient see his or her belief was learned and not intrinsic. Abuse can also create a distorted sense of importance. An undisciplined child may grow into an adult believing him- or herself entitled. Such a person may not hold that the rules of the social world should be followed and may cause his or her own special grief to others. In view of this evidence, one conclusion is hard to escape: morality, the sense of self, language, and social values are learned and incorporated into the substrate of brain and mental functioning. Nurture and nature clearly work hand in hand to produce a person.

If nature and nurture cannot be disentangled, any consideration of life and the human condition must include both aspects as much as possible. We can construct a linear scheme in which a line represents nature at one end and nurture at the other. Along this line nature and nurture interact. Only at the extremes does one completely dominate. For example, at the nature end are the contours of the nose, the size of the body, and the propensity for certain diseases; at the nurture end, we can see language, moral values, level of education, and many attitudes. But as you move from one end to the other, nature or nurture takes precedence to varying degrees. As science grows, our understanding of the dominance of one over the other will change. For now, we are tied to the knowledge available and confess to this limitation whenever an argument about the human condition is proposed.

A sensible life becomes more likely when it takes these issues into consideration. Extremes of opinion, with their coloration of certainty, are inimical to any life with meaning. A life of balance in all things, Aristotle's ideal (eudemonia equals the golden mean), provides the grounding. Like all value-laden concepts, *sensible* and *balance* are not easy to understand and even more difficult to defend. One cannot escape the irony of this, especially in a book where the essence of the work rests on the value of *sensible*. My confession is that I realize I'm writing inside a fault line and accept the limitation of this "defect in logic." I can only hope that the overall argument finds a resting place in readers' minds and may enhance their thoughts in some small way. The *balance* being sought depends on the perception of the reality in which we humans reside. Delineating this reality as best we can becomes the purpose of this work.

What I have undertaken is basically a long editorial meant to express the opinions I've gathered during my life to those interested. Where footnotes or reference notes are demanded, they will be included. Otherwise, the reader's indulgence is required. Nearly every point made is controversial and deserves discussion, if not outright disagreement. No opinion should be allowed to stand unchallenged. Yet, I do believe in all the positions I take, and this is an honest (as honest as I can make it) rendering of my perspective on life and living.

Though this book is an editorial, it's the result of years of reflection and professional experience. Psychoanalysis may not be perfect, filled with philosophical dead ends of dubious value, but it opened my mind to the way the brain works. The unconscious is real. People truly function without awareness of a great deal of their emotional beliefs. There are personal currents in everyone outside of awareness. Denying these currents and the way they operate on people's decisions is a fool's way of living. Unfortunately, many of these rivers of unknown thought are instrumental in life decisions. Learning what these are and how they operate is one of the great benefits of being a therapist. I am indebted to all my patients who taught me nearly everything I know. The discipline of psychiatry broadened out this knowledge. The wisdom acquired from this combination of therapeutic engagement and psychological knowledge makes up the foundation of this book. I'm sharing with you what I've learned with the hope the information will make your life easier and more sensible.

The opinions offered may bother some people on both the conservative and liberal side of the aisle. I can only hope that due consideration and reflection will be given to the ideas themselves. I am not interested in controversy, though I have no wish to avoid it. I'm interested in how to live a sensible life. I think I have some valuable ideas to share in this regard and hope you will feel the same.

PART 1

RELATIONSHIPS

• • •

MOTHER-CHILD

CASE REPORT: A FIFTY-FOUR-YEAR-OLD CAUCASIAN woman made her appointment with a shy, whispery voice. She accepted the time offered without consideration to her own schedule. The history she gave was without much color or feeling. She was married to a harsh and critical man who told her repeatedly that she was wrong and not fit to be the mother of their now grown son; moreover, he told her that she did not know how to dress. None of her complaints related to this. She was frustrated that the boss she had at her long-held job as secretary was similar to her husband. She felt depressed and was having trouble sleeping. Her question at her first session had to do with why she was so unable to cope. "What is it about me," she asked, "that makes me so inferior? Am I really so bad?"

It is surprising how easy it is to forget that we are all born. This over-whelmingly important fact, so obvious to all, is rarely part of our daily awareness. The implications are enormous. We are animal forms. Even if we bestow upon ourselves the embodiment of a god, our animal form remains a powerful element in how our lives proceed. Just to get a sense of this, let's consider the meaning of beginning at birth.

Even as a zygote (a fertilized egg, that fascinating product of the join-ing of the father's sperm and the mother's prezygote egg), relationships begin. Because we develop in our mothers' wombs, we are responsive to their environments. We grow in the context of their bodies, affected by their responses to the world, including their relationships with our fathers, and amid all the biological determinants. We are wonderfully whole at birth. Yet, we arrive with this physical and psychological con-nection between ourselves and our parents. This unappreciated union has complex social antecedents. At birth, the way in which our parents joined to form us, the prenatal history that brought them together, is crucial to our understanding of ourselves. The focus in an adult appre-ciation of our lives is too often the story of our experiences after birth; what led to that life is often equally valuable. However, we will wait for that discussion and begin at the onset of the new baby's story.

Birth is the mother's declaration of her wanting a child. She may want enthusiastically or half-heartedly, but delivery is the fact she held out for the nine months to let her offspring live. This begins the mother-child experience for better or worse. We sense this initial commitment to our mothers, and it has a narcotic effect on our thinking. From this, we later feel an attachment that denies the mother's personality, denies the meaning of the birth from the young delivering woman's point of view, and undermines a realistic assessment of origins. This feeling is enhanced by the first years of living. The mothering figure (the biological mother or another) is devoted to the existence of the child. Diapering, talking, playing, and in all ways aiding in the child's development creates a powerful aura of dependence and attachment. This also creates a mental state in which the mother is powerful, dominating, and unswervingly correct in all things. When mothers are troubled, frightened, confused, abandoned, or the product of an aversive home life, that fact becomes lost on the child, leaving it awash in confused conflict between the power of the mothering figure and the sense of unpleasantness the disturbed mother conveys.

The problem can be very subtle. Psychiatric documentary movies of mother-child contact make it clear that the woman holding her infant can project a sense of uncaring or lack of interest in the child. Studies reveal negative emotion is felt by the child and can cause the onset of irritability or even ill health. There is no way for an adult to take back these experiences later, yet they may play a profound role in the individual's sense of self and self-worth. This relationship begins outside of the consciousness of the grown-up investigating adult and yet is crucial to his or her life. Some awareness of this aspect of mothering can help in the adult's adjustment to living. Often this early experience can only be derived when the patient recalls later childhood memories.

I must emphasize the importance of the hypnotically controlling effect of these first months. By the time we've grown to age four years or so, when our memories usually begin, the power of those months of mother-child interaction have been enormous. We thus acquire our sense of the world as hospitable or alien; we feel we can negotiate or learn that negotiation with large powers is impossible; we gather a sense of humor and play, or we feel that spontaneity can be hurtful, even deadly when the parental figure is a threat. More importantly, we learn for the first time what it's like to relate to another person.

Our relationships and our philosophy regarding relationships begin at this time. If we're loved and feel comfort with our mother (and later, our father), we assume we're valuable and others should find us so. We see the world as welcoming and wanting. We assume at a party or school that others will want to be with us. This foundation given by loving parents, of course, can blind us to our faults and our need to properly work the social connections in the world beyond our home. The mother-child relationship is not the only factor in this, but it is important to appreciate. The sense of a valued self comes from these early months and cannot be overestimated.

Father plays an important role by adding to the crucial one the mother has begun. His support of the new mother is essential to her feeling of well-being. This added security gives her the surety she needs to devote all her attentions to the new child. In addition, his attitudes and investments in the child are additive. The self-image the child develops as he or she matures depends greatly on the father's behavior. The parents become the first community, the cultural representatives, and the first forced adaptation for the growing individual. These early years constitute the youngster's attempts to please, adapt, and understand the social context of the family. The world of the home may disappoint, or it may be quite complex and different, but the child's principles of adjustment and adaptation derive from those years in this crucial developing environment.

All of this transpires so unconsciously that it is very difficult for the adult to see this influence. Few realize that the glass-half-full or the glass-half-empty perspective on the world comes largely from these early years. The argument has been made but cannot be overemphasized: language development and social sense are acquired largely through the interaction with parents. The parents are the template from which we judge all of our relationships. The mother-child template is the most powerful of all.

Case follow-up: the insecure woman comes from a home where her worth was not emphasized. Her parents had severe conflicts. They often became angry at her after a fight. She developed a sense if inferiority that was so ingrained that she crumbled at any criticism. Her husband and boss were continuing in this tradition, and she had no self-esteem with which to combat their denigrations. She hardly saw herself as worthwhile. Her maladjustment became prominent as she reached full adulthood and realized the succor and comfort she needed could not come from others. In fact, her immediate contacts were critical toward her, not supportive. Their condescension had nothing to do with her; their insensitivities came from a source in their own backgrounds. The patient was counseled at length regarding her need to see others as they are and not as symbols for parental harshness. She improved somewhat, ultimately divorcing her husband and obtaining another position in her company with a more reasonable executive who needed a secretary.

SIBLINGS AND SIBLING RIVALRY

Case report: two brothers were partners in an import-export company. Joey discovered his brother, John, had been secreting 20 percent of the profits into his own coffers without discussing the matter. This came to light inadvertently when the government forced a tax audit. When Joey confronted John, the latter cried, "I deserve the extra. Mom always preferred you. All my life I was deprived. I always got less than you did." Being completely unaware of John's feelings up to that point, Joey was shocked. He had often wondered why John acted hostile or irritable toward him. Joey had never felt preferred by either of his parents, and, in fact, had feelings similar to John's. He came to therapy crestfallen, seeking a way to deal with his emerging depression and anger.

There are numerous important issues derived from early childhood experiences, and we can only cover those that seem often neglected or unappreciated. One of the most salient of these, sibling rivalry, deserves to be discussed at length.

Not everyone has a sibling. The position in life with or without someone sharing the parents is, nevertheless, important. The only child has issues related to being the soul child-support of the parents. Their lives, the child is forced to think, is in his or her hands. Parents pour all of their devotion onto one child; as a result, the child often feels the burden of being special and makes adaptive adjustments accordingly, responding sensitively to the parents feelings. This life of the lonely only is not as easy as it may seem to some. The obligation to please even the most caring and reasonable of parents can be a great pressure. Only-children have spoken of this pressure to please as much as they have spoken of the loneliness felt without a sibling. Later in life, this need to make the other person content despite self-sacrifice can become a significant problem in new relationships where the need for critical scrutiny of another person is required.

Having a sibling is always having a competitor. The intensity of this can be great or small, but it always exists to some extent. Many who grow up loving their siblings deny this, but their denial flies in the face of biology. The firstborn is initially the single recipient of parental love and attention. The new sibling dilutes this love by his or her presence. In litters of lower animals, the sibling competes for food and survival. Another mouth to feed deprives the first offspring. There are many examples in nature in which the older offspring kills the younger in the survival game. Frequently, the eaglet born first pushes the second hatched eaglet out of the nest. Ecologists point out that it is difficult for mother eagles to hunt sufficiently for two offspringThe survival instinct in the firstborn bird is powerful, and the competition is merciless. After the eagletcide, the firstborn thrives.

Humans are so much more complicated, but the biological association with other animals has to be taken into consideration. The parent who doesn't appreciate this minimizes its effects and is unresponsive to children's complaints about their brothers or sisters; as a result, he or she commits a crime that results in sibling rivalry. The parent's obligation is to seduce the children into believing they are all important and all loved equally. This is often untrue, but the illusion is essential if the siblings are to grow up with a reasonable amount of amity and self-worth. Even the unsuccessful effort to convince the battling children they should learn to stop fighting can be salutary. The worst parental behavior is to ignore the rivalries altogether, leaving the children to their own adjustments. The result is often an enmity existing under the surface that often leads, many years later, to the pain and suffering of the entire family. Many an inheritance has been fought bitterly by sibling claimants more because of the rivalry from their childhoods than because of the wealth in the estate.

Sibling rivalry is often at the heart of decisions made on a political level, and the root of a politician's social behavior may reach far into individual history, even close to the time of one's birth. Battling over inheritance is merely one example of this. Wars have been fought because the intransigent style of a leader is based on his or her sense of entitlement formed early in childhood. Believing him- or herself to be put aside by the parent and replaced by a sibling, such a person grows up feeling resentful of others, sensing he or she alone should be in the spotlight. If he or she gets into a position of power, this unyielding conviction creates an attitude that can be destructive to all others who come across the leader's path when those "interlopers" are unswervingly and irrationally perceived as implacable competitors.

Shakespeare's *King Lear* is the quintessential play about the animosity among siblings. Edgar was assailed by Edmund, both sons of Gloucester, King Lear's trusted sidearm. Lear's daughters, Goneril and

Regan, ultimately annihilate each other in rage at their father's preference for their sister Cordelia. Cordelia dies struggling to save her father.
She is a tragic figure who never understood the importance of her sibling rivalry. As always, Shakespeare is impressively understanding. His
play makes clear the power behind this battle is irrational sibling rivalry.

Those who think the battle between cousins, such as in the War of
Roses, is not about siblings should expand their metaphor. Sibling rivalry may not account for every dictator who acts maliciously toward his or
her people, but its roots can be found in the histories of many who have
made their kingdoms miserable. People in power often see the world as
inimical to their position. Stalin, for example, saw everyone as a brother at the nipple, and his resulting paranoia governed Russia for many
years, causing the murder of millions of Ukrainians. Sibling rivalry is an
often unappreciated part of the world's social history.

Parental ignorance, therefore, can be the seeds of world conflagra-
tion. Certainly, it is an oversimplification to blame history on parents,
but it would be equally foolish to ignore their contribution. Indeed, the
putting aside of parental factors in the creation of human history in
favor of geopolitical and national variables is one of the great errors
historians make. In fact, we can see the results of sibling rivalry (and its
corollary, sibling acceptance) in the stories that unfold throughout the
world in which we live.

THE SENSE OF SELF

*Case Report: Mary Innes telephoned for an appointment, but upon hearing the
recorded message, hung up. After trying again, she happened to catch the doctor
in and asked him if he had time to see her. He agreed he did and offered her different appointment times. She picked the first one without considering any incon-
venience to her. During her first session, she explained that she had an inferiority
complex. She always believed herself as not as attractive as other girls and felt her*

husband was better than she in all things. In fact, she was quite attractive but clearly did not take care of her appearance. She complained that even her children made fun of her, telling her she was too scared of things. She should be braver.

There is a reigning debate in psychology over the development of the self. How do we know who we are, what makes our identity, and how this contributes to a person's worldview? A child is born with a genetic endowment consisting of intellectual, emotional, and other neurological gifts. Certainly these are factors in the development of a person's identity. Despite these genetic endowments, genetic and experiential, the sense of self largely grows out of the learning experiences a person has while interacting with his or her environment. Exactly how these two large variables operate is the subject of many books and unending debates. The interaction and weighing of environment- and nature-given qualities are the uncertainties. The single confidence is that the interaction is crucial.

A seemingly simple example can illustrate the nature-nurture combination. Every child is born into a language environment. The child learns the language of the parents, who usually represent the language of the culture in the community. The genetic endowment is the ability to learn this language. Nature is represented by the ability to learn; the language represents the adaptation of the receptive biological child to the world.

Another example is imprinting. Konrad Lorenz, one of the early students of animal behavior, designed an experiment in which he had his newly hatched goslings follow him in his gray rubber boots. The image of the boots had been imprinted on the learning birds. Their biology impelled the birds to follow the first figure seen, usually the goslings' mother. Nature, in Lorenz's case, was fooled. If Lorenz had not fed and cared for the hatchlings, they would have died, thinking the boots were the mother. A film documenting this phenomenon, many years after Lorenz's first discoveries, shows the goose hatchlings, now adults, flying near the light aircraft of filmmakers. These filmmakers had also imprinted the geese, and they induced the birds to fly beside them wherever they went. When the birds migrated, their journey was documented as they accepted the mechanical aircraft that accompanied them. [1]

Humans undoubtedly have some degree of imprinting, though its power is coopted by the massively developing brain and language. Imprinting probably plays some role in the power of the parents and their ability to overwhelmingly influence children, without question, until their adolescence. The power of imprinting also contributes to our sense that child molestation and other abuses are so harmful to the developing human being.

Children left without parental care are damaged forever in their lives. Numerous studies, beginning with those of Rene Spitz, John Bowlby, and many others, make it clear: early childhood health and identity depend on significant parental involvement. Children left to nurses or other somewhat distant or uncommitted caretakers suffer immeasurable harm. If the first two years of life is subject to the neglect of caretakers, the effect is often severely deleterious, even if these children are then brought up by attentive parental substitutes.

Aside from this initial meaningful deprivation and its permanent effects, there are many in-between examples. In parent-child studies, mothers are filmed looking away from their held infants as if they feel uninvolved with them. These films, used as documents of early childhood care, are then compared with filmed evidence of later development of the children. The diminished social skills present in the subjects illustrate how maternal indifference affected development years later. Mothers who have poor relationships or no relationship with the child's father often express resentment toward the preverbal offspring. This

---

1 *Winged Migration*, Jacques Perrin, documentary film, 2001.

maternal attitude is strongly felt by the child, influencing later world-views and self-evaluation.

In the eighteenth and nineteenth centuries, there was a popular interest in the feral child, one brought up, somehow, without a parent. Often seen as a wild child of the woods or forests, such a creature was romanticized into a kind of Romulus, the wolf-nurtured founder of ancient Rome (who, by the way, murdered his brother, Remus, in sibling battle over a decision regarding the building of Rome). Rousseau's "Noble Savage"—the man of the "free" world without the encumbrances of civilization—and his treatise on the education of Emile gave free reign to the idea that the "natural" child would be emotionally healthy once he or she reached adulthood. The evidence is in. This fantasy is pure nonsense. Whether a vole, a rat, a macaque monkey, or a human, the mothering experience is crucial to health, good adaptation, and a sense of the good self. No wolf could provide the necessary nurture.

Not only is the sense of self derived from this crucial developmental time, but so too is the ability to relate to others. The original world as seen through the early functioning eyes of the newborn is felt as welcoming or alien depending on how the newborn is held, talked to, played with, fed, and cared for. Even diaper changes are a communication between mother and child. The child doesn't yet "know" it is experiencing love or disinterest or even dislike. Its cognition is still dependent on brain neuronal development. Yet, the child "feels" the positive or negative. The so-called colicky baby is now understood, in part, to come from the nervous, insecure mothering figure. The developing child is not merely an unfolding genetic message. The developing child is part of a dyad with the mother, a real world representative. The mother represents the language of this world, its customs, and its optimisms or pessimisms. The child imbibes this with the breast or the bottle, how it is held, how its needs are met, and the melodies of its mother.

Some studies have shown that personality qualities may be genetic, independent of environmental influences. Identical (monozygotic) twin studies have shown that a large part of the style of a person's interactions with others can be determined by DNA. Whatever the power of this possibility, the conclusion should not be drawn that DNA is all that matters. If identical twins separated at birth both enjoy the same kind of music, or if they both draw well or even choose similar spouses, this does not mean the maternal dyad is unimportant. There are so many factors that make up a personality that the scales or observations suggesting a genetic component to life's behaviors can only make up a portion. Certainly, DNA is a major power, but so is the maternal dyad. DNA has been shown to alter its output code based on signals given from the world in which it resides. Life is a mixture of experience and DNA, and this mixture has just recently begun to be clarified.

There is, then, a reasonable position to take regarding the sense of self and the life view of an individual. This view incorporates the genetic contributing factors and, of equal strength, the developmental factors. These developmental factors consist of the maternal dyad and the family environment. On a slightly lesser scale of important influence are peer relationships and actual life experience.

There remains the surprising fact that sociologists and psychologists have only recently started to use the developmental history of a person to explain poor political behavior in leaders, serial killers, and criminality. Even a cursory inspection of criminals (those in jail allowing themselves to be evaluated) shows these people come mostly from very troubled families. All attempts to show that criminality is largely genetic have failed. The overwhelming evidence is that issues of trust, distrust, violating the rules for personal advantage, and feeling no discomfort for the suffering of others comes from family dysfunction during development.

You might think, after reading all this, that parents have to be perfect. This is not so. Nature, interestingly, gives a wide latitude for healthy behavior in the parent, and the child is also often surprisingly resilient. A troubled marriage can be filled with conflict while the child is loved by both parents. This is certainly experienced by the child, but, more often than not, this does not disrupt the offspring's sense of self or his or her perspective on the promising life ahead. If the parents are loving toward the child while fighting with each other, the child will probably grow reasonably well. Amazingly, the tiny creature distinguishes between the marital battles and the fact that he or she is cared for by the combatants. The variety of adaptations available to humans is startling. This makes everyone hesitate to write off a troubled family and assume no good can come to the children while they live in that environment. Within certain limits, a lot of trouble can occur without the young individuals being severely psychologically injured. The ranges of adaptations youngsters make never cease to amaze me. However, the important point is to never minimize the significance of this process of development. If we are to understand relationships and the people in them, we must take into consideration these developmental issues and the environments in which they occur.

Parents and Children

No one can exaggerate the truism that parents live through their children. Reasonable and healthy parents who bring a child into the world see the child as part of themselves and, more often than not, want to give this new being every opportunity to become a person "better than themselves." This parental bonding is crucial for development but brings with it special problems.

The narcissism that is necessary for any child to evolve into a self-caring individual also creates a potential threat, causing some children to feel so entitled and egocentrically deserving as to complicate any integration into the family or the wider community. Discipline and limit setting becomes the medium through which this is curtailed. It is crucial children realize that there are some things that cannot be done for them or by them and that they are *part* of a family and not the *center* of it. Being made aware of this mitigates the deleterious effects of the feeling of entitlement. Without this training, children (or their adult selves) tend to feel unreasonable frustration; they grow up seeing themselves as significant and deserving to such a narcissistic degree that it becomes impossible for them to live meaningfully with others.

If the sense of self evolves from the mother-child dyad, how does that affect the child's view of the world? The mother's position is so powerful, as she exerts imprinting and an emotional tone on the mind of the infant, that the child is unwittingly influenced. The child is at his or her mother's mercy and can do nothing at this early stage to offset what happens to him or her. Only much later in life can he or she reinterpret these experiences cognitively in an attempt to make a change in him- or herself. The child is in a long-held state of receptive immaturity, with no conscious idea how the mother's interpretation of the world is different from one that might prove healthier. When the child becomes an adult, he or she has no memory of these first four to six years. During this time, the child's state of receptivity is so complete that the values incorporated become dominant in the child's preverbal experience.

Youngsters accept values laid down without assessing their merits. Moreover, the natural egocentricity of the child makes an individual interpretation of the mother's idiosyncratic values far from any consideration. Rather, the child interprets the world only in terms of his or her own behavior and does not even realize the mother is implicated and part of the child's thinking. The tenaciousness of this belief that the self is responsible for everything is so strong that when the child reaches maturity, he or she has no awareness that the world was interpreted in this fashion.

This peculiar mental state is clearly demonstrated when the adult who was given up for adoption as an infant cannot shake the belief that the adoption occurred because "there was something wrong with me. There was something missing in me." A person can go through marriage and parenthood with a sense of inadequacy, never realizing that the origins of these feelings are in the ideas surrounding his or her adoption. Helping people realize there was a history prior to their birth, and that the history played a major role in the decision to give them up for adoption, is an important challenge when helping adopted adults whose sense of inadequacy has affected their lives.

Abused children also demonstrate a similar misinterpretation. The abused child typically interprets the parental abuse as a punishment he or she earned. The child had made life difficult for the parent, and the parent's behavior is understandable to him or her in those terms. When you ask a ten-year-old what he or she thinks of his or her mother or father beating him or her so severely, the standard reply is, "I must have been bad." The child has no ability to evaluate the parent as a separate entity, as someone with his or her own problems that led to the abuse. Psychologists term this strange self-referential behavior as childhood narcissism, a propensity to see the parental and outside world only in terms of his- or herself. The world, to children, has meaning only as it relates to them; there is no history, no causality outside of that selfish domain.

This childhood narcissism prevails in many adult lives, where the sense of self and worldview is too much based on the child's view. The employer who fires the adult is often not seen as a person with his or her own problems. Instead, the employee takes the firing as personal, feeling a sense of failure or inferiority. The suffering party does not think he or she has been let go because of issues, behaviors that evolved from childhood in the employer.

In intimate relations misinterpretations can also occur. Attitudes and other behavioral complexities are independent of the person who is treated poorly with extreme inconsideration. This thought does not occur to the suffering recipient of this behavior because of self-referential thinking. There is the debilitating effect of a self-referential interpretation of the world. This idea that "it must be me who caused the trouble" persisted into the observer's adulthood. The child within dominates the misbehaving loved one, creating the problematic attitudes and behaviors. Similarly, the child within dominates the recipient partner in the blinding effects of childhood narcissism.

While dating, a girl may feel the boy isn't calling back because there is something wrong with her. "He doesn't like me." The possibility that the boy may have problems with relationships does not arise because of the self-referential thinking so common in young people.

The ability to see beyond childhood narcissism is something a good parent can help develop. A growing person can be taught that everything does not revolve around him or her, and the world has its own issues. However, this is rarely part of the foundation parents impart since they are often unaware of their own distortions. Leaving behind the notion that a person is the center of the universe is not always easy and requires increased humility. The person must understand his or her limitations and have confidence in his or her strengths. Each of us must make a realistic evaluation of ourselves within the context of the greater world. This is frequently not a perspective anyone can readily achieve, but should be viewed as part of the highest level of maturity.

THE ADULT CHILD

Long life has led to increased concerns between parents and fully grown children. Though children as adults have completed their growth and fully identify their own characteristics, they still may require some guidance. The twenty or more years between parents and their offspring have allowed for maturity and experience in the developed parents, and this can prove useful. Conflicts between parents and children should be resolved by the time the son or daughter has children. The resolution of these conflicts is most important and renders old age more salutary.

Grandparents are often reluctant to give advice to the new parent and feel a natural distance from the son-in-law or daughter-in-law. This should be bridged when significant problems arise. The balance between not interfering and giving good guidance has to be kept in mind. Taking a position of either extreme is a mistake. Opinions about child rearing, job problems, and money should be offered to willing and receptive children. The advice should be conveyed in a tone of concern and helpfulness, not criticism. If the message is clearly in the spirit of helping, most young adults will welcome the advice. The tone of condescension is always off-putting. The rule is to give advice in the style and tenor one would use for a good friend, always showing a regard for the thoughts and feelings of others. If advice is refused, there is no recourse but to retreat. Advice not wanted is never effective. This is why a convivial relationship between parents and children is extremely important.

Difficult adult children present a special problem. The conflicts between parents and children derive from childhood. Parents are often surprised by the resentments their adult offspring express. The resentments date from childhood. Parents may not appreciate the long-held negative feelings their children continue to hold inside. Dealing with issues many years remote from these resentments clouds their connection.

Addicted adults often hide deep feelings of neglect. The addiction can be an expression of self-abuse, representing their sense of failure and their feelings of unimportance to the parents. Drugs are used to hide the painful mood. Avoiding painful moods is the first cause of addiction, but there is also the deep sense of failure toward the parents in the adult now grown. This is coupled with a belief that the parents are profoundly disappointed in them. Without an appreciation of these elements in the relationship, dealing with conflicts satisfactorily is doomed, and problems can never be resolved. There is even less hope of a comfortable working family relationship.

Life problems may not be in the immediate conscious, but they emerge at unpredictable times when associated events stir them up. Celebrations such as birthdays or Thanksgiving get-togethers with the family are often seedbeds for old, unresolved issues. Some extraneous attack between two siblings at a dining table is usually based on conflicts long simmering and never addressed is always an unpleasant surprise. The immediate cause is rarely obvious. Old conflicts are in play, but they are not apparent to anyone. Trying to resolve them openly at a more congenial time, especially if the people in question are very willing to alter their views, is the best approach. Creating an atmosphere where the problems are hidden or little discussed is tantamount to creating a deterioration in the overall relationship.

The worst approach to adult children problems is to deal only with the obvious manifest issues: child rearing, money, who comes over for Christmas or Chanukah, and so forth. These conflicts hide long-standing unhappiness between parents and children. Without going beneath the surface of the obvious, nothing can be done. An angry adult child is certainly upset over the patently obvious matter that cannot be resolved, but there is almost always a long-standing hidden conflict that must be identified.

Certainly matters such as child abuse and neglect cannot be solved by any kind of talking. These are the horrors of childhood. If the parents are responsible, the best step toward resolution is confession and the asking of forgiveness, and there is no certainty the adult child will respond positively. These are severe ruptures of the parent-child relationship. Surprisingly, many parents and children can gain a new footing through acknowledging their problems. Some can never do so.

DATING AND MARRIAGE

The biological drive to mate is powerful, and few resist it. Those who do resist often suffer. Studies repeatedly indicate that the sharing of life with another encourages longevity and increased health. These comments apply to homosexual and heterosexual relationships. Companionship is powerful, meaningful, and probably healthy, and its effects on quality of life are not to be overestimated.

With this in mind, it is not so surprising that dating, that insistent process whereby we try to meet the person with whom we want to share our lives, is of overriding importance. Dating develops in adolescence and matures in early adult life. Despite the dating imperative, few involved understand the process. Finding a companion becomes the work of instincts and hopes, and usually there is little rational thought involved. Typical individuals look for someone to "like them." If they find this person, the decision is made. The desired person is eagerly hoped for, and our seekers wait for the return of affections. In film and daily experience, the girl or boy goes on an approval campaign. "Does he think I'm pretty? Does she think I'm good looking?" What is really happening between two prospective partners is quite different.

There is a better way of viewing what's happening. Two people wanting a companionship should not be merely looking for someone to like them, but for a match. This match means that the two are close in their views and feelings. Compatibility, mutual appreciation, mutual sexual attraction, and similar education and interests are all among the issues being paired. If someone does not like you, this, contrary to popular thought, does not mean you are deficient in any way. It means there is not a match; the two do not share a sufficient number of qualities.

So much wasted pain and suffering go into feelings of being spurned, unloved, and rejected. In *The Sorrows of Young Werther,* Goethe tells the story of a man who is repeatedly told he is unloved by the woman he desires. Ultimately, he commits suicide because he cannot tolerate the rejection. The woman in question is described as vain, entitled, and insensitive; in contrast, Werther is sensitive, caring, and estimable. Goethe got the point and shares it with the reader. This suicide is a tragedy because it's based on the feeling of rejection from an unworthy match. Werther's insistence that his worth is correctly assessed by the rejecting woman, his belief that he is therefore undervalued, and his feeling that she is the only match worth living for, places him in the unnecessary and therefore tragic position of deciding he must end his life. This, of course, is a false and fully unjustified act. The tragedy comes from the false egocentric belief that blinds Werther to the truth that he should never have loved this vapid woman in the first place.

If only the "young" Werther hadn't reasoned in such a "young" fashion; if only he had better control of his childhood belief that the world centers around him and that its rejection of him means he is useless for life; if only he had correctly perceived his presumed love as the unworthy woman for his affections, which she decidedly was.

In the dating world, a woman or man, boy or girl, must appreciate that a failed match means nothing more than the two were not suitable for each other. Suitability depends on like-mindedness, and this is not easy to find. The dating enterprise must be viewed as an exploration in search of the right combination, not a testing ground for individual value.

The issue here is psychological compatibility, although there is another view, that of the evolution and the viability of the species. In terms of pure survival of animal types, copulation is the only goal because it leads to a new human. If humans were merely animals with no conscious mind, this would be the only purpose of mating. Certainly this is clear when we observe nonhuman animals. "Chemistry" then reigns supreme. In naïve adolescents, this can often be the predominant motivation in pairing. However, the limitations of this bonding are clear to everyone. The mating desire of the teenage girl forces on her the wish to be found attractive and loved without reflecting on the full meaning of her actions. This is why we try to protect our youth from their inclinations until they can seek a mate with their higher reasoning in place.

With higher consciousness operating, a person can make a choice with more awareness of the future that might result from the wrong choice. Chemistry no longer applies. On the individual level, evolution is not a consideration. The only important thing is a relationship in which individual satisfactions are supported, and the children are reared by two partners that like them and each other. The purpose of dating is to guarantee this.

MARRIAGE

Marriage occurs when two people want to share life together. Both have different histories, different personalities, different perspectives on how to live life, and different life goals. The two come together with all these differences and expect to live compatibly. This illusion is created by the positive feelings they have toward each other and the powerful effects of biological sex. The honeymoon is dominated by these compelling feelings. After vows and ceremonies are over, the work of living together begins.

Marriage has phases. These can be grouped in many different ways, but they will always include: (A) The early getting-to-know-you period, (B) the development of children period, and (C) the empty nest period. Throughout these times, the handling of money, sexual matters, and the day-to-day issues of adapting one to the other are the predominant concerns.

As mentioned, marital partners come from different backgrounds. Each has a unique history. This history has effects on the manner of each partner's behavior. For example, someone from an abusive childhood will have difficulty interpreting his or her new spouse. Growing up with abuse numbs a person to his or her own emotions. Talking about feelings in an abusive environment is dangerous. Children learn quite early to keep thoughts about feelings to themselves. By the time dating and marriage connections occur, this style is firmly embedded in the mind. For this reason, marrying someone from an abusive background handicaps the relationship. The partner who suffered past abuse is going to have difficulty sharing and working through differences. A normal person expects the partner to talk about disagreements, and an adult who was abused in childhood is generally inhibited from doing so. The result is frisson and disharmony between partners. Psychological therapy may be needed to help the abused person. Otherwise, the marital relationship can come to a standstill and severely hurt the healthy partner.

Couples with different levels of education, different religious beliefs, different ethnic backgrounds, and even different national identities present with special issues. The worst position to take is to ignore these matters. They are salient to the relationship and must be addressed. The details can be enriching or destructive, depending largely on how willing each person is to talk them through. When people assume that differences will take care of themselves in time, the hurts accrue and eat into the relationship.

A less obvious conflict revolves around the issue of money. Decisions on how money is managed can be very destructive. Couples should be as frank and open as possible about who will manage the finances, whether bank accounts will be shared, and how the money is spent. Some couples remain secretive because each wants a little private financial turf to call his or her own. Secrecy is not necessary. Each should discuss having a discretionary income as well as the marital income. There are many ways to do this, but bringing financial matters out into the open and deciding how to operate the business side of family is key. Anything less breeds uncertainty and potential deceit.

Marriage success ultimately rests on resolving or working through these and other differences. Having children may put aside the immediacy of these settlements, but it never dissolves the necessity. Many couples hesitate to fix these issues early in the marriage and are haunted by them later.

Nothing rises above the importance of giving the partner the feeling that he or she is loved. Each desperately wants to feel special in the other's mind; each wants to know he or she is completely able to depend on the other when in need. This has to be communicated frequently and meaningfully. Simply helping with small matters like picking up the other's napkin, opening a door for the other, and helping to carry packages can communicate care and concern. The marriage feeds on this. It is the bedrock of every successful marriage, and the lack of this message is the shoal on which most marriages wreck.

When there are conflicts, each must ask what specific issues in the psychological nature of the spouse may be contributing to the problem. Understanding the partner's background, the forces that molded his or her personality and the traumas that might have affected him or her, is crucial to any understanding of that person's behavior. Often, a person is not reacting to his or her partner but to some issue that stems from his or her troubled background, an issue that has somehow been triggered by the partner. Taking all behaviors from a partner as personal and directed at the sufferer is not a good idea. When bothered by a partner's behavior, it is always a good idea to think in two ways: (1) How is this behavior connected to me? (2) How is this behavior connected to his or her background? Despite the feeling that arguments that often occur in marriage are personal and directed, many battles are fought over background issues about which one spouse is unaware.

It is important to differentiate between symbolic conflicts and substantive conflicts. The first occurs when a marital issue stimulates unresolved problems in the partner, and the issue is a symbol of that conflict. The second is about marital disagreements or problems that simply need to be settled between the partners. Symbolic fights are the larger problem and require the insight and understanding of each person. Refusing to look at symbolic conflicts in all their meanings leads to very destructive altercations. Two well-meaning people can nearly always resolve substantive disagreements.

Case Report: a husband becomes unduly angry because dinner is not ready when he comes home from a hard day of work. His wife, too, has worked hard, but he feels an implicit agreement that she will have dinner prepared for him. She feels hurt that he refuses to understand her explanations of the day's schedule interferences and fights back. He overreacts to her and throws a plate onto the floor. The child in the high chair cries out, and the husband runs out the door in a rage. What the wife and the husband don't realize is that this battle is being played out on his history. He was neglected by his mother and is overly sensitive to any neglect by others. He always reacts excessively when he feels neglected. This problem was never resolved and continues to play out in his marriage repeatedly. The wife wants him to appreciate her efforts to please him and cannot understand the degree of rage he exhibits.

There are current issues and historical issues operating here. It would be easy for the couple to miss his historical problems by emphasizing the simple conflict of the wife not having dinner on the table. This seems like a lack of appreciation one has for the other, but it truly harks back mostly to his history. The real provocation comes from his inability to understand why his wife's not having dinner on the table is not a result of maternal neglect.

SUMMARY OF NONSEXUAL RELATIONSHIP ISSUES

Relationships are at the core of life for everyone. However, they are never easily understood. This is because each person brings his or her history into the connection. There are three compartments that need to be kept in mind: (1) The nature of each person (2) the compatibility of the couple and whether they match or not, and (3) the importance of resolving the practical problems of living together and compromising on differences to manage themselves and the family. History is always playing its role in relationships. So is good will. If the relationship is seen as valuable, the couple will work out the issues while keeping in mind the three compartments of difficulty. The key to marriage, then, is negotiation, negotiation, negotiation. If the couple does not talk out the issues, all will fail.

The couple's relationship depends on this mutual quest to understand each other and make adjustments for the marriage mission. Here the mission is the marriage, the mutual agreement to live together. There is, of course, the sexual side of marriage. Sex can be a part of the problem and, if not salutary, eat into the relationship. Sex deserves to be discussed separately.

SEX

Does anyone doubt the power of the sex drive? It's possible to be celibate, a virgin for life, and still be significantly affected by sexual feelings and inclinations. Mendicant monks who flagellate themselves to dispel the fantasies of sexual congress testify to the sex that they cannot ignore. The energy that troubled people expend to unite sexually despite major characterological differences that separate them testifies to sex's power. With such a powerful biological inclination, is it any surprise sex occupies a considerable part of anyone's life? The strangest part of this is that no one can explain it. Knowing we have sex organs and sex hormones goes merely the smallest distance to explaining why a man is fixed on a woman's body shape, or a woman is possessed with the idea of enjoying a man's penis. These impulses are part of what humans are. Alluding to evolution, the importance of reproduction and the universality of every animal's drive to participate in sexual joining does not really explain why members of the human species are attracted to one other in the normal course of events, and that's that. DNA notwithstanding, sexuality is a mystery.

It is important and essential that sexuality be acknowledged. A heterosexual may find homosexuals' interests repellent or inexplicable, but this same heterosexual cannot explain the attraction between him or her and the opposite sex. Whatever the fundamental hormones, genes, or pheromones that attract, they operate outside of the will of any individual.

We are born sexual, and there is no escape from it. A man stares at a woman's cleavage. A woman stares at a man's crotch or his torso. A homosexual finds another homosexual attractive—a "turn on"—and the cause is of little significance, except to researchers. Society may place a value on this behavior, good for some, bad for others, but that evaluation is self-serving and has no meaning outside of social mores. There is no universal sex morality that is absolute for all time and all places. Every culture and every period of history has made their assessments, and they vary enormously.

The fact that most beings are heterosexual does not mean the value of heterosexuality is automatically higher. This conclusion is an individual one. More does not mean better, as obesity makes eminently clear. More heterosexuals might be better for a species to continue its existence, but that does not translate a homosexual being into a bad or immoral person. This kind of ethical thinking will be discussed later, but for now, suffice it to say that sexual morality is largely arbitrary, however many fall on one side of the issue or the other. Gender orientation cannot be legislated.

The sexual act is a major enjoyment of humanity (and, perhaps, of all mammalian life—or even of all animals that join sexually, including,

for example, insects and snakes). Whether all animals get the same pleasure humans do may be argued, but let's agree that humans like it very
much. Because they like it so much, they do it a lot. Sadly, many do not
get the pleasure from it that is available because their psychology gets
in the way.

It is possible to put rats in a cage with a tiny wire implanted in a part
of their brains now called the pleasure center (specifically, the nucleus
accumbens). If we send just the right amount of electrical current to
this center, the rat will perform some behavior—say, tapping a lever—in
order to keep the charge coming. Every time the lever is tapped, the rat
gets the charge into his pleasure center. It has been shown that rats will
starve themselves to death rather than stop the behavior: it feels that
good.

Clearly, as enjoyable as sex is, it must be kept under some control.
It's one of the appetite behaviors, eating being another one. All humans want to participate, but participation must be balanced with other
needs. Teenagers are especially at risk for overindulgence and must be
helped through their "burning" years to safely become adults who use
sex more wisely.

It is the teenager who attempts the argument that "there is nothing
wrong with it, so why should I stop?" The pre-AIDS seventies and early
eighties were full of this perspective, so the issue should be addressed.

There is no solid, defensible argument that would convince a floridly
sexually active person to desist. There are some less-than-solid defenses,
however. Observation strongly suggests that unconstrained sexual intercourse with a number of partners who have no emotional involvement
with each other leads to feelings of emptiness and a devaluing of the
persons. It would seem that sexual intercourse is a highly personal and

meaningful behavior, despite the feelings of experimenting teenagers and young adults.

James Bond, a good example of the individual who does not attach much personal significance to his sexual behavior, is portrayed as aloof, uninvolved, and unresponsive. He can get any woman he wants, but after he does so, he is left only with his dedication to the British Secret Service. The one time he had an emotional reaction, the writers killed off the woman to allow him to maintain his character as distant and self-centric. In the James Bond world, women are mainly for sexual pleasure. Bond is an alienated gloss who is dedicated to his job, not to a life with meaningful relationships. Interestingly, this is how many bachelors turn out: distant, avuncular with limited family connections, and alone.

In dealing with patients, there is impressive evidence that people feel better about themselves if their sexual activity is limited and is applied to partners that are steady and well-known. The one-night affair is not satisfying for most, even if it seems to be at the beginning of a sexually active life. People want to know with whom they are having intercourse; they want the other person to care about them and to share in a dialogue surrounding the activity. Males and females do not want sex to be automatic; they want it to be part of the ongoing discoveries usual in a developing relationship. Although through a long marriage, a couple may desire occasional automatic, unemotional sex, these couplings remain a spicy element in a foundational relationship, merely a part in the larger world of courting-like, caring sexual encounters.

Married couples will say that the sex is better when the relationship is good. It is often surprising how many don't appreciate this. Couples in therapy will declare their sexual relationship has waned while oblivious to the reality that the insipid quality of the sex they have been having is a reflection of marital conflicts. It is most difficult to enjoy naked congress after unpleasant words or serious fighting.

All humans vary in their sexual readiness. Both men and women change sexually through the month. For women, desire is clearly connected to the menstrual cycle. For men who don't have such an obvious biological clock in operation, the same rise and fall of desire is easily established. Without sex, men will have spontaneous erections and an increased sexual fantasy life, causing them to reach out for sexual relations with the available female. Though people are widely aware of this, partners rarely discuss it. In the best of sexual marriages, each partner's sex drive is acknowledged, and both partners are sensitive to the other's needs.

The style of sexual activity is entirely up to the couple. Each member of the pair has to learn not only what he or she likes, but also what his or her counterpart likes. Clearly, there are sexual acts that one may want to avoid that the other wants to include. For the relationship to proceed successfully, this problem must be settled. The worst outcomes occur when the issues are ignored. Compromise may be required. Extensive maladjustments from each individual's attempt to please must be avoided, or the result will be a persistent disintegration of the relationship. I cannot repeat enough that no relationship is without compromises. It cannot be ignored that each person comes from a vastly different historical background. Sometimes a couple's incompatibility was evident from the beginning of the relationship but became most obvious and painful through their sexual difficulties and undeclared differences. If compromise cannot be reached, the couple may have to separate.

An important distinction must be made between fantasy and the sexual act. It is possible for a couple to have a very healthy sexual life while having fantasies that do not include the partner. Some feel this is a betrayal of the partner and have considerable guilt. The partner may feel the betrayal and react with excessive anger. However, couples can have excellent home relationships and sexual activity and simultaneously use movie figures, mutually enjoyed pornography, or other fantasies to enhance their personal response. Betrayal is not the only interpretation of this. One can view it as a little mental help when required. Neither member may want to know that the partner is thinking of someone or something else during sexual intercourse; there is no obligation to tell. Many a successful marriage has been mutually enjoyed while an image of a movie couple's sexual success has been in one of the partner's mind. The marriage may be no worse off, especially if there is healthy mutual regard and care in every other sphere.

Sexual behavior is a complex subject, prone to being laden with self-serving values. It is more useful to see sex as a special category of behavior and appreciate the importance of finding the right balance between two different people who have two different stories and who require original thinking to work out differences. With this open-minded approach and the belief that what works indeed works, plus the appreciation of the importance of compromise, couples should find their sexual lives healthy and enjoyable.

Breaking Bonds: Divorce, Death, and Infidelity in Marriage

• • •

Divorce

BREAKING A RELATIONSHIP IS PAINFUL. The loss of a relationship is the loss of a commitment, a guarantee. The mutual feeling that the other person is available for care, affection, or need is one of the most comforting in a life where uncertainties prevail. Each partner incorporates this feeling and connects it to his or her sense of personal importance. The value of the other becomes a survival component of the self. When the relationship becomes so toxic that separation and divorce are necessary, the feeling of loss of self and the other person combine. The result is an overwhelming feeling of despair. There is no surprise that the resulting feeling is one of betrayal.

One feels the assurance and presence of the significant other. There is an implied and written guarantee in marriage, and this agreement is comforting. A person's spouse gives the feeling of security necessary in an insecure world. When this consensus is lost or tossed aside, the disruption in the sense of well-being is profound. The aggrieved person feels failure or self-denigration. Sadly, as the breakup continues, in order to regain a feeling of rightness in the self, each defensively attacks the other. The unconscious wish is an attempt to show how the other failed in the contract. Laying blame helps reconstitute the health of the self-view.

It is rare that each member of a couple sees the disintegration as a result of an imperfect match in the first place and not necessarily the responsibility of any member of the pair. As with all interpersonal conflicts, there is little to be gained in trying to convince the other person of his or her defects. People will defend themselves to psychologically conserve their senses of self. The criticized naturally tends to counterattack for just that purpose. The most difficult maneuver in this situation is to sit back and ask if compatibility can be achieved or maintained at all.

Beyond the primary consideration of compatibility, couples often face serious and burdensome secondary considerations. The couple considering divorce must take out the balance scales. On the one side is the unhappiness in the marriage and what that does to children. The other side of the scale weighs how divorce affects the children. Divorce breaks up the family, but constant emotional excitement or marital outbursts affect the development. One must decide which is worse.

The health of the person primarily responsible for the care of the children must be considered as well. If constant strain causes deterioration in health, divorce becomes more inviting. After all, if the caretaker's health is seriously affected, the children can suffer. The choice is between two undesirables. Determining which one is truly worse for all concerned determines the opposite. If it is worse for the children for the couple to stay together, then separation is warranted. This decision is one of the most difficult in life, and there is no fully good choice.

The decision to maintain the marriage has to include the possibility of improvement. Spouse therapy or marital therapy many alter the playing field and allow the relationship to continue. If the spouse cooperates and tries to improve the marital home, all attempts should be made to allow this. The moment a couple breaks a relationship is not one to be entered impulsively and is a time for serious deliberation and careful consideration.

DEATH

The loss of a loved one, especially someone with whom you've spent the better part of your life, is always traumatic. Whether the relationship was good or bad, death is never a neutral experience. In some cases, death is a relief. Perhaps the spouse was sick for a long time, a severely unpleasant person, or someone who narcissistically did not allow the survivor to follow his or her own life inclinations. Each handles the death of a spouse according to his or her personality and life philosophy—people have life philosophies even when they are unaware of them. Conformity, rebellion, dependence, and independence are all based on viewpoints that come into dramatic play when a spouse dies.

In general, adaptation to the death of a spouse is maximized when the deceased was loved, when the deceased was appreciated with a full realization of his or her limitations, and when the survivor has a strong sense of independence. The marriage should have been mostly a pleasure. The couple shared mutual respect, and the survivor has a clear sense of him- or herself and the ability to take care of him- or herself.

Problems arise when excessive dependence on the spouse was the style of the marriage. The survivor's feeling that he or she cannot live without the deceased and that an essential part of the survivor has died is a sure indication of maladaptation to the loss. Depression, with its attendant sense of hopelessness and helplessness, often results. Life originally had meaning only in the shadow of the spouse. Now that the shadow is lost, meaning is lost with it. If the survivor cannot find solace in children, activities, or a new relationship, he or she may not survive.

Statistics have supported the idea that spousal deaths within a short period of time after a spousal loss are not unusual. The healthy marriage is one in which each person is comfortable without the spouse but enjoys the marriage for its benefits. When the marriage takes over the sense of self and a person is only comfortable in the marital bond, loss through death creates a pathological state for the survivor.

Grief over loss is normal. Long-standing relationships are not easily relinquished. There is always a recovery period in which the survivor makes a major life readjustment. This time is not easy for anyone. However, the new situation is much more manageable if the individual knows him- or herself, understands clearly what an independent life should be like, and came from a marriage that was built around the mutual respect of two independent people in a lifetime contract for mutual satisfaction. If marriage is, however, a long-standing solution for an unconsidered life, if the spouse is the replacement for a self never fully realized, and if there are no other interests or distractions that fulfill a person, the adjustment can turn into a disaster. During the marriage period, it is essential that each person develop him- or herself independently of the other while sustaining the marital bond. No one wants to lose the person he or she loves more than anyone else in the world, but should it happen, there should be, inherent in the self, the ability to live independently.

INFIDELITY

The fundamental principle of relationships is that if the relationship cannot be salvaged and the bond cannot be retained, the connection dissolves because of incompatibility, not because someone is bad, excessively disturbed, or inadequate. Two people agreed on the marital contract in the beginning. Clearly, each wanted the relationship and wanted it to work. The state of mind at the beginning may very well have been different than at the time of fissure. The maturity and worldliness of each may have been undeveloped, but his or her sincere wish was to make this agreement to live together work.

At the time of marriage, it is rare that a couple fully realizes the financial and work issues that will arise. The two may very well underestimate the change in feelings brought on by children. Sustaining a marriage with these extra relationship concerns is quite different than sustaining a marriage when being together as a twosome is the prominent focus. The compatibility at the beginning may be fine, while compatibility in the middle might falter.

So many marriages end with rancor. The energies of both parties are spent trying to demonstrate the breakup is the other person's fault. When partners are immature, each fears his or her own vulnerability and works hard to pass the blame for any impasse onto the other person. Sometimes this can be the result of subtle but powerful childhood developments. In jealousy, for example, the concern over the other person's infidelity results from an internal fear of inadequacy that the jealous person may not understand. The drive to prove betrayal is a defense against the inner anxiety that the betrayed person is inadequate in some way. The feeling can be translated as this: "If he or she cheats on me, I am a deeply flawed person. I am essentially no good."

Occasionally, the fear of inadequacy can be so severe as to cause violence against the person committing the infidelity. The male may interpret a perceived inadequacy to keep a woman happy sexually as a symptom of his own homosexuality, certainly of his own inadequacy as a male. Most of the time, the jealous suspicions are based on a sense that the betrayal was of his sense of self. The jealous person feels his internal self-regard and respect is threatened. The anger centers on the feeling that the psychological contract has been broken; the suffering partner therefore believes the person who breaks the contract should be exposed and hurt in a similar fashion.

It is almost never the case that these interpretations by the betrayed are accurate. Most extramarital affairs are caused by the unhappiness of the persons engaged, sought as a relief from the sad state of the marital relationship. One partner usually communicates this unhappiness at some time, while the other partner ignores it. When the betrayal occurs, the shock and dismay is partly because the offended partner has already worked hard to hide the truth of the unhappiness in the relationship.

Before an affair is discovered, it is of utmost importance to discuss any problems in the relationship when they arise. Issues should never be put aside. The couple must compromise as much as possible and work hard toward a compatible resolution of differences. Jealousy and infidelity are clear indications that the marriage is not working. Betrayal is a word used by the psychologically blind partner who feels he or she is the victim. The truth of the negatives in the relationship is almost always evident but sadly denied.

If the marital conflicts cannot be resolved, the couple has to consider divorce. It must again be emphasized that betrayal and infidelity come from a break in the psychological bond, not from someone being bad. If the relationship can be saved, it will be saved because problems in the relationship are addressed and resolved. The betrayal is a symptom of problems between the couple, not the main question that has to be addressed. The loss of trust is the result of strife. It is the strife that must be the focus, not the trust. Trust will be reestablished as the grievances are aired and solutions found. If a partner has been denying the problems, once the infidelity is discovered, certain questions must be raised: Why has this happened? Can each person alter his or her behavior to reestablish the original passion for each other? The worse alternative is to simply find blame without being able to discuss matters beyond the need to condemn the other person as "cheating."

The male who catches his wife cheating and then kills her is behaving on the surface of his awareness. He wants to show rage at being victimized. Below the surface, in his unaware unconscious, he is saying, in effect, "You have made me feel inadequate and frightened. I must treat you as a venomous creature who means me harm. I must protect myself by eliminating you. This reassures me that I will never have to recognize my own weakness. By making you bad, I remain undiscovered."

It is not at all unusual for many marital partners to project their feelings onto their spouses. The spouse then unwittingly behaves as if in a kind of movie created by the partner's feelings. This story is very convincing to the projecting spouse who sees all the confirmation of his or her suspicions, even though the evidence is created by him or her. When this occurs, the victimized spouse has no recourse. He or she must either get the partner into therapy or break the relationship. There is little defense against a person operating outside of awareness who makes up stories and then confirms them by interpreting the spouse's behavior through the lens of his or her own fantasies. Trying to convince the partner in a discussion of the unfounded basis for the claims is futile. The comments will simply be twisted against the person in order to protect feelings of vulnerability that are entirely unconscious.

Though betrayal is one form of defense against marital misery, there are others. For example, complaints against a partner may find their roots in issues in the complaining spouse's childhood. A severely critical woman who is never satisfied with her husband can very well have her attitudes derive from a childhood where a father was rarely available or overly critical. Women who have had traumatic sexual experiences can see sexual inadequacy in their husbands who would otherwise, by others, be found quite adequate. A husband may see his wife as a domestic failure or a failure as a mother because his own mother was neglectful. Projection of this type is a common defense in people who do not know how their own pasts play into their current judgments.

WORK

Relationships are important in the workplace. This is an understatement. What is a surprising fact is that many do not appreciate it. There is a tendency to see the workplace as simply a place work is performed satisfactorily so that one can obtain a reward in the form of pay. Certainly, the worker must have the skills to do the job demanded and show up regularly to do it. These basics are, of course, present in any job. However, the work is done in a human environment. People interact, and the way they interact plays a large role in quality of life, the quality of the work environment, and the quality of the work performed.

A person's ideal work environment includes work within that person's skill set, a supervisor who is reasonable and understanding, and a sense of enjoyment derived from what the worker is doing. It would be useful to take each of these factors in turn.

People who are hired outside of their skill range are reluctant to lose their positions, despite the obvious incompatibility. In our capitalistic society, wages not earned lead to a difficult and undesirable life. A worker, once hired, will desperately try to perform to keep the job. If the skills required are simply not present, the supervisor must then take on the unpleasant task of terminating employment. When a problem arises in the assessment of the employee's skills, trials are devised to determine an employee's abilities. These trials should be assessed objectively. When the worker clearly cannot master the requirements, she or he should be given every opportunity to find other work. Nothing is more toxic to the work environment and overall morale than abrupt termination. Those in charge of the workplace should avoid this as much as is possible.

Supervisors (or "the bosses") hire and fire. They evaluate work performed. They also must perform and are answerable to the business or to others who have a higher status. The boss, then, is a person in a job. He shares with the worker similar characteristics: family, ambitions, and the need for approval. The boss is a human being with a history, and it is forever surprising how often the boss is denied these qualities in the estimation of his or her employees. Whatever aura the chief's position might have, he or she remains quite vulnerable and prone to error just like his or her underlings. The boss has a childhood, life aspirations, and relationships outside of work that may or may not be satisfactory. He or she makes judgments based on these factors, but whatever problems the boss has are made opaque to many by the power of the position—the aura of presumed excellence often disguises deficiencies. The employee is usually unaware of these realities and feels he or she has little choice under the usual work agreement but to comply. Of course, complying with arbitrary and hurtful demands is exceedingly stressful. This stress cannot be eliminated with psychological wisdom, but it is ameliorated by being aware of the human being behind the position of authority.

The most stressful part of employment is rarely the work itself, especially in the growing service industry. What is more hurtful is the deleterious interpersonal relationships in the office. It is a rare work environment in which the sense of fair play and a reasonable interest in the worker guides behavior. More often, the workplace is a world of bitter rivalries, feelings of vulnerability, fear of financial disruption through unemployment, and, in many cases, significant and dominating injurious psychopathology.

The employee must be vigilant and fully aware of these factors. He or she must never set blame on the self when the pathology of the boss or fellow worker is a major factor. Not recognizing that pathology is operative is the number one failing for people who suffer the stress of poor interpersonal working relationships.

Aside from tyrannies in countries throughout the world, there is often the tyranny of the workplace. Most workers want to do a good job. Most employers want fair work for money paid. These are obviously the basics, but all too often there are pathological types in the job arena who cause unnecessary grief and pain. The threat of discharge is the axe these despotic bosses hang over the heads of employees. The worker then operates in the shadow of misery. When a supervisor uses this persistent cudgel to force work done in his or her fashion, the battle is waged and the victory is won, but the spirit is lost. As a byproduct, productivity is ultimately lost.

Loss of morale and increased stress are poorly appreciated causes of underproductivity. The dominating supervisor who is more interested in control and power than productivity is causing problems outside of his or her awareness. The results are blamed on the employee. What is not usually appreciated is that the productivity problems stem from the supervisor's problematic psychology and not the worker's work.

Of course, the problem can be occurring on the other side as well. The employee may have significant background psychopathology. Psychological problems coming from childhood maladaptation can affect the worker's ability to deal with authority and make working within the constraints of a regulated environment difficult.

Psychopathology causes problems no matter who is suffering from it. Since behaviors are caused by issues and history unrelated to the work environment, the misinterpretation that the work setting is a factor leads to poor resolution and a persistence of production impairment. The importance of recognizing psychopathology cannot be overstated, but determining that someone is behaving outside of reality is not always easy. A sense of the usual is essential. Most people try to conform to a work environment. The façade of comfort is the norm for American culture, and any deviation from this is noticeable. A boss or worker who is clearly irritable, depressed, frequently absent, satisfied with inadequate work, or distracted is probably suffering from internal issues. These can be the result of the negative work environment or personal demons. In either case, the problems have to be addressed.

Once a troubled person is labeled as such, the focus of concern is turned toward that problem and not the work. The employee who sees the boss as a psychologically impaired person realizes that the issues have little to do with him- or herself, or with the work alone. The employee then has to decide if a transfer is possible or if leaving the workplace is necessary. The issues relate to the psychopathology, not to the criticism, unpleasantness, or the poor evaluation the employer might have given. It is most important for the employee to separate him- or herself in point of view or attitude from the troubled employer. The internal message is that it is not the work performance or the worker's personality that is causing the trouble; it is the supervisor's internal pathology.

In a similar fashion, the psychological problems of the employee may be the underlying factors in poor performance, not the ability to perform. If a personality problem creates a diminished work output, the employer must address these issues and make sure the assessment is independent of the ability of the worker to do the work. If the employee does not find solutions to the issues impairing work, dismissal may be necessary. In a fair and caring workplace, supervisors give employees every opportunity to resolve their internal conflicts. It is only after all these opportunities are exhausted that release from employment should be considered.

Competition creates conflict. It is a rare individual who can appreci-ate the talents of another and be comfortable. Employers who view the employee as critical, talented beyond themselves, or a threat to their position can become difficult themselves, fearing the talented worker will usurp them. A worker must realize when the supervisor has these feelings. As long as the position is necessary or desired, he or she has no choice but to downplay his or her abilities and call attention to them as little as possible. Realizing there is a competitive attitude is essential for survival; ignoring it creates a peril to the position.

Projection is a psychological defense mechanism that often oper-ates in the real world and certainly can be a factor in the workplace.

Individuals have internal lives and bring these lives to the office. If a worker suffered from sibling rivalry issues in childhood, he or she will often project these issues onto fellow workers. Rage at a brother may become part of rage at a colleague, although there may be no indication the problem arises from out-of-office issues. Abuse at home can result in the worker seeing the supervisor as an attacker when, in fact, he or she is only supervising. A sense of disrespect in the office can arise from a sense of disrespect at home. Projection confounds interpretation of problems in a relationship.

The issue in any conflict reduces to a few questions: Is it me? Is it him? Is it her? Is it the situation? Not asking these questions when office problems arise leads to idiosyncratic beliefs that may have no basis in reality. Always, a worker must step outside of the conflict and determine where the essence of the problem lies.

Money

After body and verbal language, money is the quintessential psychological means of exchange. Money can't compete with words when considering how humans communicate and conceive their world, nor can it compete with body language and gestures. However, money is a close third. The psychological meaning of money is often overlooked. Every time one person gives a dollar to another, meaning is involved. The other person may deserve the dollar because of work done (justified and agreed upon service), because of a loan made (trust), because of need (helping another), because of saving (responsibility toward self or family for the future), or because of obligation (commitment to another). The list goes on, but the meaning is clear: money is emotional communication.

Of course, as an economist will instantly attest, money is also a means of doing business; a way of keeping society in food, water, and home;

and a substitute for the ancient bartering system. Of course this is true. Money can be discussed and explained with no association with feeling or human understanding. People can draw charts that show goods required over price asked, market trends, or debts incurred; none of these need include the emotional meaning to the large numbers of people involved in the transactions.

When considering individual lives, the psychological meaning of money becomes prominent. How a person plans his or her retirement depends on how that person views his or her lifestyle. Whether someone loans money to another person depends on the relationship involved. If a child asks the parent for a dollar, the parent may give it with or without an expectation of certain behaviors from the child. Self-esteem is far too frequently attached to the amount of money a person has. A big house means to some that he or she is successful. A Lexus outranks a Toyota (though, indeed, made by the same company). Airplane business class is for the successful. It is nearly impossible to consider money without the human meaning attached.

Everyone must make peace with money. This is not easy. For most, appreciating the limits of the budget, planning for the unexpected, and saving are difficult. In late adolescence, a young person must decide what kind of life he or she is going to live. Will he or she pursue a career with large remuneration or a modest job with limited income? This depends on the person's view of him- or herself. Can that person compete in the marketplace? Does he or she have the ability, the attitude, the temperament, and the fortitude to go for the big money?

None of these are easy questions to answer. What is ironic is that the psychological importance of each person's relationship to money is often avoided, glossed over, or denied. Money is the "filthy lucre," the passion that leads to doom. Silas Marner suffered because he was "greedy" but maladapted to social living. The moral tale told by George Eliot is clear: if you live for the money beneath the floorboards, you are not fully part of the world. Pip in *Great Expectations* was successful because his kindness with the gift of food led to the kindness of an escaped criminal who later gave him the wherewithal (money) to succeed. Dickens is fully aware of the sensitive contradiction. Money is dirty and dangerous, but it can also be used to save a lost life. This partial recitation of the complexity of money can be extended to many examples. Suffice to say, life without money is impossible. Whether it is good or bad depends on situations and people.

Money is a serious consideration. It is a part of life. Food, shelter, environment, social situation, and money are all part of a person's essential concerns after self, family, and society. Money becomes a part of how life will be lived, and there is no automatic advice on how to value it. The way money is used is based on people's character, who they are, what values they have, and at what level of life (socioeconomic) they expect to live. People with simple needs require less money. Those who want children, wish to travel, or enjoy a meal out will need more. The middle class learns to live in the middle. In short, money is important and psychological. Avoid its meaning, and the consequences can be impressively painful. It is neither good nor bad, just as a tree is neither good nor bad. It simply is and must be used wisely.

THE SELF

The self may be called the soul. The soul may be called the self. This tautology is usually not appreciated, and discourses on the soul as understood in religion are legion. The sense of who we are and the feeling that this self-sense can be immortalized through resurrection under the tenants of some religions is the origin of the concept of soul. Descartes struggled with this in his mind-body duality, a concept created to deal with the difference between the animal and the spiritual being. This duality helps prevent all humans from feeling merely like animals. The body is the animal, it is argued, and the soul is the essence of who we are. Descartes's struggles and the religious myth surrounding what happens to the soul after death have everything to do with how people conceptualize their souls. "May your soul burn in hell!" This curse is made in many horror movies. "The devil has your soul" is a statement many mothers make when frustrated with the antics of their two-year-olds. What we are all talking about is the sense of who we are and all that makes us sentient beings.

Is there a soul? Is it better to argue whether there is a self that can sustain itself beyond death? The short answer is no. The self dies with the body, and all evidence that can be garnered indicates it does not continue. It does not persist in some ethereal space after the corpse is reduced to bones. Of course, this becomes a religious argument, and there is little purpose in trying to win one of those. Each religious person argues from his or her intense convictions that protect him or her from an alternative worldview. This will be discussed under the chapter titled "Religion"; for now, let me indicate my position: the soul or self is a biological or social product that lives within the body, develops over everyone's time of life, and dies when the body dies.

Many of you readers will want to continue this debate, but the primary purpose of this section is not religious; my purpose is to discuss the psychological meaning and significance of the self.

Sigmund Freud wrote volumes on the self, calling it the ego. The ego, he said, was the mediating part of each person, the part that helped the mind deal with the world outside the mind. The ego mediated between the realities of daily life and the inner world of the person's thoughts. It was a great reality tester. If the world suggested the person was good or bad, the ego would help him or her decide which was to be believed. A part of the ego, the superego, mediated the mediator by giving it values it could depend upon.

From Freud's point of view, this was the self. Of course, this is a nifty and enticing conception that remains open to question. Is this concept of the self sufficient? Is it useful? The answer for both questions is sometimes yes and sometimes no. Nevertheless, this concept of the self has value and holds truth, and its merits must be appreciated. What Freud is saying is that self, the sense of who we are and what makes our sense of uniqueness special to us, is a complex psychological construct of which only a part decides what's real and what's to be discarded. However intriguing and captivating this concept is, it remains a fraction of the picture.

One cannot deal with the self without, sooner or later, coming up against the intellectual struggle between nature and nurture. How much of the self is biological and genetic, and how much is learned and familial or relationship based? The story of psychology is the story of these questions. Since the nature-nurture controversy is ongoing, we cannot draw a pie and section off the percent of contributions of nature and the percent of contributions of nurture. The problem arises when someone takes too severe a position, positing that this or that feature of the human is all nature or all nurture. We can draw a spectrum line, putting nature on one end of the line and nurture on the other end. All elements of self can be placed somewhere on the line, nearer to one end or the other. Intelligence can be placed near nature, but not all the way next to it. After all, being endowed with genetic intelligence can be thwarted by malnutrition and a toxic living environment. Many a genius has been brought up in a deprived home that denigrates using the very skills that have been provided genetically. There are brilliant people who dig ditches.

Similarly, a person who has inherited average intelligence from genetics can become a professor at a university or capable of tasks because he or she was encouraged from birth to delve into these matters. Most of anyone's success in academia is due to diligence and emotional stability, not native intelligence.

Intelligence, one of the most highly inheritable of mind traits, can have significant nurture features. Personality, the day-to-day style in which a person interacts with everyone and everything, can have both genetic and environmental qualities. Some have argued that temperamental differences can be seen in newborns. No one has argued that the language used in everyday speech can be seen in newborns. Just as we discussed previously, the ability to learn language is genetic; the language used is environmental. If you are born into a Croatian family, you will speak Croatian; if you're born into an American family, you'll speak American English. Even if you're bilingual it's because that's what was spoken at home. Nature and nurture operate together in most things, and both have to be considered in every determination of self.

Since the genetics of personality, intelligence, and language have barely been delineated, there is little more to say. We are held to the idea that these qualities in all of us exist with strong genetic contributions alongside crucial influences from life experiences. Though this seems easily agreed upon, in practice many people underplay the nurture part. When we try to understand the nurture that operates in the formation of the self, we often run into insurmountable difficulties.

Like language, self begins at birth and develops in part from the influences of the immediate environment. The most powerful elements in this environment are mom and dad. The newborn is held, suckled, talked to, touched all over its body, and admired or rejected by the parents. Though mother is extremely important in all this, father is as well, and his importance increases as the child grows. Learning language and learning the self happen simultaneously. The mirror is held before the child so that he or she knows who he or she is. This mirror is largely in the form of mom and dad. Slowly, year after year, the child learns the rules of the world through the parents; he or she learns the rules of eating, sleeping, regulating (the bowel, the daily light-dark cycle, and so on), loving, hating, tolerating, and sharing.

The child is also learning whether he or she has importance or value. A loved child knows the self is important. The rejected child knows the self is problematic. All of this happens to such varying degrees that the influences are not even recognized. A father who yells at his three-year-old daughter for waking him from a nap is telling the daughter that he is more valuable than she and that her behavior can bring violent reactions from male figures. The father may forget this, but the child does not. His rage at her then colors her feelings of herself and affects her future, including her social interactions. Similarly, a child who is not disciplined sufficiently (disciplining children is always a balancing act between too much and too little) may grow with a sense of entitlement and a lack of frustration tolerance. Sibling rivalry unchecked by caring parents easily results in a sense that all relationships are a battleground; this is a battleground in which the grown-up is filled with maladjustments. Now relationships are misinterpreted based on the wars formerly at home.

The many permutations of maladjustment of the self cannot be covered. Multiple variables operate inside every life experience. A mother can be mostly loving but occasionally become rejecting. This can be handled in different ways by a naïve child. The child's genetic make-up results in an unpredictable self-development. Correctly predicting outcomes, even when knowing the family factors involved, is nearly impossible. There are many stories of people coming from terrible home environments who were, nevertheless, able to find some stable and meaningful life for themselves. The details from these histories tell of a more complex outcome, with nestled problems hidden within the overt success. Rarely is the case that a criminal does not come from a difficult and dysfunctional home. Tap the shoulder of any incarcerated criminal at random, and most of the time you will learn a history of a miserable and maladaptive home life. Even though every life cannot be easily explained, the basic principle that nurture plays a major role in self-development is impossible to dismiss.

The self comes from genetics and lived history. The genetics gives intelligence, temperament, resilience, and style. Experiences with parents, peers, and people in the real world gives language, style, feelings of inner comfort or disturbance, a sense of value, an appreciation of others, ability to handle authority figures, and an ability to interpret the world. This listing is clearly not exhaustive but demonstrates the primary principle: you cannot ignore historical background when trying to understand the manifest behavior of anyone.

Self, then, is the total sense of who you are, where you come from, your context in the world, a feeling of your value, your abilities, your aesthetics, and your place in any relationship. Self has everything to do with feelings, but it also has to do with logic and thought. Feelings and thought, cognition and conation (a medical term for feelings or drives)—all of this has multiple determinants.

The world of humanity, which always wants to protect itself from discomfort, tends to minimize nurture. A young man is listless, exhibits few interests, does not keep a job easily, lacks a sense of future that any ambition would protect, and becomes an object of criticism. The critic does not notice or care to notice that the young man's father is of a similar nature, and his father and family do not value ambition at all. The criticism falls on deaf ears because through most of the man's life, he never heard such concerns. He is simply being what his family taught him to be.

A young woman feels her boss is overbearing and harsh. The boss struggles to help her see the work has certain demands and is part of the employment. She insists on seeing him as someone who is harassing her. There is no opportunity to appreciate that she comes from a family with a harsh father. This father was so critical and unbending that he turned his daughter into a person who feels no authority is reasonable. She now loves her father and has no recollection of how difficult it was to be his baby daughter. She cannot comprehend the reality of the workplace because employment is viewed through the eyes of a child feeling her father cannot be satisfied. The reality of the workplace is hidden by the unconscious effects of her father.

The self becomes a compendium of all these experiences. Though the previous examples are designed to show the negative side of self-development, many positive examples abound. A woman with confidence, a sense of purpose, a feeling or regard for others, and a strong propensity for solving problems under adversity probably comes from a family that taught these virtues through the behaviors they showed to the young woman. She learned from the beginning of her existence that her mom and dad could be trusted, disagreements could be negotiated, and she was valuable no matter what slips and errors she made.

The self cannot be easily summarized, but the idea can be elucidated. Self is often confused with soul, and the idea that it can be stolen or signed away is a product of Christianity, which espouses resurrection and the continuation of the spirit after death. If language were used in the place of the word *soul*, one could translate that language. The word for *soul* is the essence of a person. The word is imbued with the idea that an essential part of us lives after death. Despite this meaning, it's as if the actual *word* may go to heaven and be welcomed by Saint Peter. *Word* can be given away to a Beelzebub, or it may be lost by corruption. There is the feeling that the word indicates something, but it is an abstraction of language and has meaning only as a word given our needy significance. Of course, none of this makes sense. The soul is not a palpable thing. The presumption that it has more material meaning than the presumed meaning is wrong. A simple word cannot be this transformative. The word *soul*, then, has historical and current beliefs attached to it. For many these beliefs of an after-death-spirit-of-the-self continuing to exist is a belief that gives material essence to the word. Yet this is a belief in an abstraction and has the meaning installed into the word, no more.

Sadly, the soul, as with so many important ideas, is merely a construct, a product of language and a yearning for immortality. Its meaning and its significance is merely a part of human language and human desire. How many penitents have beaten and suffered themselves because they feel their guilty souls will go to hell if they do not punish them in this life? *Soul* as a word has no more meaning than this.

Therefore, the captivating quality of the word *soul* rests on its cultural history. Soul has no meaning outside of this religious culture. When speaking of others and trying to understand their natures, it is more useful to refer to the idea of self, the more complete meaning of a person outside of his or her physicality.

LIFE PHASES

Before leaving our discussion of some of the permutations and problems in relationships, a comment has to be made about human behavior at different phases of life. Though this has been alluded to in sections above, the emphasis here is on differences at different times of development.

There are three easy divisions or life phases: childhood, adulthood, and old age. Of course, the boundaries of these categories are not well marked (one usually runs into the other), but they are useful in developing an overall perspective. Childhood can be subdivided into infancy, early childhood, and late childhood (or preadolescence). Adulthood can include adolescence proper, young adulthood (perhaps twenty to thirty), and full adulthood (perhaps thirty to fifty). These are suggested divisions and not meant to be the final word. They are guide points only and designed to foster discussion. What is addressed here will not be all-inclusive. Many excellent books have been written looking at each of these divisions in great detail. Here, the outline is merely a format in which to make a few points about individuals' lives.

Infancy is a largely devoted to the biology of our growing new persons. During this time, there is massive neuronal and body development. Though the interaction with the parents is crucial for infant healthy growth, the psychological importance of this period is weighted toward the infant's sense of well-being. Though no one has been able to measure this, it is clear from observations that children develop a sense of the world outside themselves by comfort of care, involvement of the mother through feeding, body contact, pleasant vocalizations directed at the child, and quick response to distress indicators. Many studies have shown these issues to be crucial. Children who do not get this constant quality care and positive emotional communication thrive poorly and development abnormally.

Childhood is marked by increasing communication, learning to tolerate frustration, language development, emerging motor skills, and an overall intensification of interpersonal communication. During these years, roughly between two and six, the child knows no world but that of the parents. Peers, siblings, and environment are all secondary to parental power. Mom and dad are giants with complete dominance. There seems to be a biological sense in the child that if mom and dad can't be pleased, he or she is doomed. Though the terrible twos, a time in which the child does not please the parents, are a contradiction to this, the child is exerting his or her inner needs in the face of powerful agents. Never does the child feel safe except when mom and dad make it clear there is only love and care. The frolicsome misbehaviors of the emerging child are overlooked.

This sense of the parents as tall, powerful, godlike beings cannot be overemphasized. As the child grows, if he or she perceives weakness or incompetency in the parent, that realization is a thunderclap of disappointment. The natural errors of parenthood are the seeds for the child's developing sense that the world is not as perfect as it first seemed. Parallel to this reality check is the persistent belief that a parent's will cannot be breeched. He or she is the final world on all that is. The world *is* mom and dad. Mom and dad *are* the world. All values, all instincts, and all behaviors are measured according to these powerful figures. The worth of the child derives only from the parents' value of little him or her. It is during this period and the near subsequent times that the child begins to feel important. The parent's value of the child becomes the child's value of him- or herself. This feeling of worth (or the lack of it) is indelible, carrying over into the rest of his or her life. It can be an impediment to success or an aspect of great achievements. The powerful belief in the self becomes a mysterious sense that is unshakable.

Therapists can form some idea of a patient's sense of self when they investigate the nature of mom and dad. He or she asks the question, "What were mom and dad like? Do you remember their attitudes? How did they treat you?" The therapist makes a logical inference leading to the opinion that a difficult and incommunicative parent during adolescent or late childhood (memories usually available to all but the most impaired) probably behaved in a similar fashion during the earliest years as well. Sharing this realization with a patient is enormously helpful. Insight into these influences helps most people understand their own feelings about themselves. They begin to see where their beliefs about themselves came from.

The key point here is that the way someone feels about him- or herself, that person's self-worth, is based partly on experiences of early childhood. This worth is not an objectively derived estimation of value. It doesn't come from comparing the self with others; it is a feeling obtained from parents during early growth. The newborn child is an organic being with genetic endowment, but how he or she feels about him- or herself is not based on that; it is based on how the child is treated after birth.

So many walk the earth feeling good or bad about the self and believing their beliefs are clear and concise. They do not appreciate how derivative and cultured this belief is, how much of it comes from chance, and how much of a role the parents' attitudes played in the creation of this belief. A genetically talented musician who is told by her mother that she really doesn't have that talent will believe the teaching. She may never become a musician, something at which she might, being genetically endowed, excel at and enjoy. Nurture at a very early age plays a vital role in everyone's feeling of worth later on.

The adolescent's entrance onto life's stage challenges all the presumptions the child had. These presumptions came from the parents, but now the world begins to work on them. The self-doubts of a teenager occur on the well-established bedrock of childhood-parent experiences, but they occur in most people nevertheless. The adolescent becomes very sensitive to peer opinions. Even though healthy parents have given their children a strong feeling of worth, they are not sure how the rest of the world sees them. A thirteen-year-old pubescent girl wants to know if she is attractive, likeable, desirable, and "normal." The thirteen-year-old boy wants to know if he is acceptable to his peers and lacks the qualities that single him out as deficient. Concerns about sexual identity emerge at this time.

Sadly, this interaction with the world is not at all an accurate indication of reality about the self-regarding youngsters. An adolescent is an emerging skill form, someone whose abilities are yet to be tested. The peer group is in exactly the same position. In fact, group clinging is an indication of this need. The group gives a false but powerful reassurance that a teenager is acceptable and all right. Teenagers do not see this clearly at all. This feeling of insecurity, often fed by childhood lack of nurturing by the powerful parents, can lead to tragedy. Internet suicides in which the vulnerable child interprets e-mail assaults as valid are good examples of this. The problem most likely comes from early parent-child deficiencies. The victim's self-sense is impaired just enough so that the peer attack wreaks its damage.

The world is certainly not what the adolescent sees. Her or his true value is in no way reflected in the opinions of others. The social view is dependent on the trends and values of the moment, a kind of compendium of group tendencies that has nothing to do with the young person's actual abilities or worth. The late adolescent has passed through this gauntlet of peer nonsense and is ready to face independent life.

Going to college, getting a job, and living in an apartment away from home are all part of the separation of person from parent. This transition is meaningful for everyone, and it is always a challenge. The strength to withstand the realities that the world imposes on a person comes from proper nurture at home and a strong reality check on the peer pressure of adolescence. The more parents and friends made it clear that the child can do as well as any human being, the more the young adult can put his or her hat in the ring and tolerate the slings and arrows of early adulthood.

During this time, teachers, employers, and friends will continue to help or hurt him or her as he or she naturally struggles to find his or her bearings. A teacher who discourages (because of the teacher's own personal issues) can either be accepted or rejected. Discouragement by an excessively ardent college professor suggests someone who has his or her own agenda. The recipient has to decide if the criticism is worthwhile or a reflection of the critic's need. Likewise, a friend who urges drug use can either be listened to because of the need to belong or put be aside as having poor judgment. Adaptation depends on good sense and the feeling that one's own thoughts are as good as or better than anyone else's. This crucial period depends on all that has gone before, and confidence is based on the multitudes of supports obtained in the recent and remote past. The more confidence in the self, the more likely he or she is to get through this testing time.

What teachers, friends, and onlookers have to say is no more than a certain view of reality and their biased perspectives; there is no validity to their claims to wisdom beyond their coveted beliefs in their own rightness. The emerging adult must understand that others acquire wisdom in the same way he or she does. The young adult must be cagey and careful with whatever evaluation is given, taking no opinion at face value—an opinion is an opinion and not a fact, and even a fact can be an opinion. He or she should never be swayed by a mere comment, such as, "I don't think you have what it takes to do this."

Adulthood takes many forms. In this relatively brief treatment, the commonplace will be the focus. The variety is extensive: the recluse, the bachelor, the family, the criminal, and the traveler are only a few examples of the way people manifest themselves in their adulthoods. Since relationships are the main subject of this section, the issue of marriage and family shall take front row.

Finding a loved one has already been discussed. The principles of understanding the nature of the other and determining whether compatibility is likely cannot be overemphasized. When it comes to finding a lifelong partner, the question should never be, "Does he or she love me?" but, "Are we suited for each another?" The "Does he or she love me?" question is always a holdover from childhood. Either it's a match, or it is not a match. Mutual enjoyment being and sharing similar values are the only criteria needed for a relationship to begin. As more experiences are shared, the feeling of love and interdependence strengthens or weakens. A boy can profess his love, believe the girl is beautiful, and act at all times in the most polite manner, but he and his partner may still be completely incompatible. Nice is not enough.

The strong erotic feeling that accompanies young adulthood is a confounding element in finding relationships. How many loves are created and sealed with that primary sexual pull? All too many connections are based on passion, not a consideration of what is required from a person when you live with him or her. This results in a delayed awareness that the match is inappropriate. We've already discussed how when children come into the picture before the incompatibility is realized, the ensuing misery can be life-altering for all.

It is certainly no easy task to determine if a match is likely or not. This takes time. Frequent dating, learning the history of a person, and sharing experiences over time are the ways in which you learn about someone. Time is a friend of a lasting relationship. Jumping into any union is a bad idea. Quick contact denies the complexity of matching and leaves no opportunity to learn about the other person. No one can find a good partner without good information. Every new relationship is an experiment. You try it, and it either succeeds or fails.

Clearly, a problem can arise when you've been "experimenting" with someone for a long time and strong feelings of attachment develop. Everyone is reluctant to break up a couple after sexual, social, and personal bonds have been established. Both partners have to ask a series of questions: Will the problems we have be relatively unimportant because the good between us overwhelms them? Will our differences eat into our comfort with each other over time? When answering these questions, it's important to realize that marriage is supposed to be forever. Forever is a long time. How significant will the incompatibility issues be over that lengthy period? No relationship is perfect. There are always differences and disagreements. The question is whether differences and disagreements can be tolerated without destroying the bond. All relationships consist of a balance between negatives and positives. The relationship will last if the positives outweigh the negatives and if the quality of the negatives is not too cancerous.

Adulthood often leads to parenthood. Some think being a parent is the final step in maturity, as the parent accepts the role of life and death over a child and determines that he or she is a reasonably competent person who can care for a child. Rearing children is a labor-intensive process. Stamina should be strong, and the work of child-rearing must be approached realistically.

It takes a lot of work to care for children. Society seems to respect parenthood, but it never seems to acknowledge the effort involved. Motherhood and fatherhood are among the most difficult of enterprises. The challenges are consistent and challenging. Whoever the stay-at-home parent is, he or she should be appreciated for the considerable work involved.

Finally, the mother and father should feel like adults. Parents are not equal to children; they are the caretakers. Children are not the same as the parents; they are a genetic combination of them. Every child has an undeveloped brain. He or she sees the world according to his or her maturation. At an early age, the environment is vague, unsure, ambiguous. The words a child comes to use after two or three years of age or uncertain, barely applicable to the world experienced. Because of this, children respond to any environment different than that of the parents and will express their personality in a unique fashion. All of this is part of the package adult parents must face.

The child is not a mere reflection of the parent. So many mothers and fathers feel the accomplishments of their children reflect who they are. This is not true. The accomplishments of the children reflect, in part, the quality of parenting. Without caring parents, the child will not have the wherewithal to accomplish his or her life goals. The confidence of the child is a reflection of the parents' love; it does not mean the parents are special or good unto themselves. The parents must get their self-satisfaction from their own accomplishments and not live through the children. When children accomplish only for the parent, they are giving up part of their developing selves. Of course, some of this happens with the best of parenting. Children are built to please their moms and dads, but this given element has to be nurtured for the sake of the child, not to feed the parents' insecurities.

The adult parent, ideally, has solved his or her own problems and sees birthing as a new step in life growth. The child is a new person with unknown qualities. The adult's job is to give unquestioning love to the child while nurturing differences that are in the child's best interest. The parental marriage bond becomes a structure in which the child learns about men, women, love, fighting, respect, and reason, but the parents' marriage has to be strong and reasonable for the child to feel this. For the new human being, the parents' relationship is the model for life ever after. The more secure each member of the partnership is, the more likely the child will be treated in a fair and reasonable way and never become the object of settling marital disputes. The child observes these models of the world and emulates them, although there is no conscious awareness of how much mom and dad are incorporated into the child.

When a baby gosling is born, the first object it sees on hatching is the mother goose. This causes a match between mother goose and baby gosling. The gosling then depends on its mother and follows her wherever she goes. Though the word *imprinting* is probably too strong for use in humans, something like this is happening to the child through parental modeling. The good parent must be aware of this and realize that all behavior, implicit and explicit, becomes part of the development fuel for the offspring.

Comfortable and fully developed adults enjoy this period of life. The responsibilities of adulthood are viewed as interesting challenges worth meeting. Marital sharing and pleasures stand side by side with parental sharing and pleasures. The individual need not neglect her or his own special interests—they become part of the pool in which floats all the family interests. This distribution of time is not always easy, but most mature adults can manage. Work, play, sex, and children are the elements of adult life. How they are managed and balanced means everything when seeking a good life.

Finally, for all of us, comes old age. Aches, sluggishness, deterioration of hearing and sight, and separation from children all emerge as issues requiring a new form of adaption. Meeting these increasing limitations is a major problem. Old age means facing death.

Old age also means all the issues of life should have been solved. If one is fortunate enough for his or her spouse still to be living and to have the mate he or she had throughout the dynamic years, one now has to come to terms with his or her emerging aging problems in the form of illness or weakness. Activities shift when what once was a pleasure is no longer possible. The mountain can no longer be climbed; the pleasure of kayaking has become unavailable because of joint pain.

If the marriage has been a good one, the adaptation to aging is much enhanced. The couple makes its adjustments and enjoys each other's company. However, the important point is that each member of the pair should feel some degree of independence from the other. The wife who relied on her spouse for finances or decisions becomes impaired when he becomes a little demented. The widow who is completely maladaptive when her spouse dies is someone who never fully developed a sense of self separate and apart from her partner. There is always grief when a loved one is lost; there is always an empty place in the heart because the lifelong companion is absent. However, there should never be a loss of self. Throughout life, the development of the self should be a top priority. A person must know his or her limits and assets. The sense that life can always be lived alone, if necessary, is the healthy position, even though companionship is both desirable and a great pleasure.

Old age is a time to foster and enjoy adult children and grandchildren. Healthy relations with one's own children are most important.

Over the years, respect and assistance for a daughter or a son goes a long way to making old age more satisfying. Grandchildren are not the grandparents' children, and all attempts to dictate childcare should be avoided. Any good advice must be given mainly when requested without overburdening the parents. Grandma's and grandpa's children were supposedly brought up confidently to find their own paths as parents. Demonstrating errors in childcare is a surefire way of alienating one's own offspring. Of course, if the relationships are strong and healthy, disagreements and contentions are not going to be disintegrative. There is no substitute for "talking it over." One of the great satisfactions of old age is the opportunity to be helpful to the immediate adult children. When the relationship between aged parents and their children is comfortable, a daughter or son asks for advice when needed. These are occasions for strengthening and securing an even better relationship. Everyone's growth is enhanced by sharing problems.

The older parent of the troubled adult child has a special challenge. Children can be overprotected. An older parent must set the balance between helping and letting the adult child find his or her own solution. The older parent sacrificing income and peace of mind for the unresponsive, maladaptive adult child is a portrait never to be hung on the wall. There is a limit to help. Exhausting income ineffectively for the son or daughter does no one any good. As with everything else, there has to be a balance between help and discipline. As difficult as this is, the older parent should keep in mind that there is no celestial obligation to drown in the lake while saving one's own. Certainly all should be done to help, short of harming the parents themselves.

SUCCESS VERSUS FAILURE

"We want you to be a success," the parent cries out. "I'll never be a success," the frustrated child laments. "I was not a success," the failure feels.

What are they talking about? What is success?

Most would agree that winning the Nobel Prize is a success. Others point to awards in their own fields, the Pulitzer in literature, or the Lasker in science, all of which imply success is certain. Getting into Harvard is a success of the moment. Winning the game is another.

We are born with insecurity and very early in life have to prove that we are valuable to our parents and our peers. The newborn is successful if he or she is healthy and cute and desired by the parents. When the sibling is born, success is dependent upon establishing his or her importance in the eyes of mom and dad. This might take the form of getting into a special class or passing a certain test or achieving a goal—all fulfill the bill.

If success is defined as above, achieving a goal, then, is easy to conceptualize. If you're running to home plate, and you get there before the ball hits the catcher's mitt to put you out, you have achieved a momentary conquest; you are successful. Society defines this, as it does so many things. Success is social, a value judgment. Since it's made by the human world, its meaning is also a derivative of the same world.

Some people set goals early in life, and when those goals are not achieved, they feel depressed. Achievement of this sort is tied closely to self-esteem. A person can evaluate him- or herself and deem him- or herself a failure. Can this evaluation be trusted?

If we look at life as a pie chart with slices representing aspects of life, then we can assess how much of that chart is related to success. For example, the chart might be divided into the following sections: family, recreation, professional life, children, spouse, professional satisfaction, income level, sense of comfort with the everyday self, sexual satisfaction, creative effort, and so on. You can make up your own categories and percentages of area to be covered. What emerges from this is that success can be achieved in any of these categories, all of them, or none of them. Professional accomplishments might be extreme while the family does not do well. The family may be happy, as we see in *A Christmas Carol,* while money might be elusive. Bob Cratchit was a very good father, but he might be considered overly attached to Ebenezer Scrooge. This attachment made him suffer monetary deficiency. His son almost died because he couldn't face Ebenezer regarding his wages. His "success" as a father and husband were made clear in the story; his failure as a wage earner was couched in social circumstances and his overwrought fear of his employer. At the same consideration, Scrooge, of course, was a fine financial success but a miserable person and a failure in the social realm.

Success is another abstract invention. It's a value made up by society to motivate and reward its members. The movie *Citizen Kane* puts the idea of success in perspective. The newspaper mogul was a huge business success but a family failure. He could not cultivate relationships for himself while he built an empire. For the movie's audience, his success would have been to have a loving wife and family. He gave everything to his passion for power, and it defeated him. If you stood on the sidelines and watched, you might have admired his money, his influence, and his status. If you were in his family, you would feel only the failure of his ineptitude.

The problem with success is the word itself. It is used to denigrate and to applaud. Its strength lies in the believer, and there really is no substantial meaning to the word. Like beauty, its meaning is only in the eye of the beholder.

TRUST

Trust of others is always earned and should never be assumed. Coming from a healthy family where fairness and mutual respect are the operational norm, it's difficult for some to see the world as it is: a place where disappointment in relationships is often the case, and where trust is frequently dubious.

When meeting someone, the possibility is to either trust the person or not. One default position can be to trust and then learn if that position can be sustained. Opposite this, the default position can be to distrust and determine later that such an attitude was unwarranted. Either position is a position and nothing more. It does not guarantee success in a relationship and certainly does not assure the other person is trustworthy.

The presumption is that one knows what trust is. This is a word with many dimensions and varied explanations. Generally, it refers to people meaning what they say and following through on what they promise. Is anyone able to perform like this at all times?

Many a parent has promised a child a toy or an event and found that he or she is unable to follow through. The child's ability to discriminate is limited, and he or she feels betrayed. Explanations regarding special circumstances often do not set aside the keen disappointment an eight-year-old feels. Does this mean the parent is not to be trusted? Hardly. The child develops a sense of trust in others if the parent is mostly dependable. It's the proportion that counts in a child's life, not the absolute quality of always bringing to fruit the given promise.

The above scenario applies to relationships in everyday life. No one is completely trustworthy, always keeping the promise and never failing the guarantee. Friends and loved ones demonstrate dependability, usually arrive on time, and regularly keep promises. Realizing this or not, people make adjustments in relationships and rarely expect every promise to be kept. What cannot be tolerated is a consistent and repeatable offense. Clearly, the only way to assess someone's reliability is in an extended relationship. It takes time to determine someone's trustworthiness.

The paranoid personality can never trust. Early life experiences of abuse and severe disappointment dictate an attitude that everyone thereafter is more likely to be hurtful and undependable. This kind of person has great difficulty determining the trustworthiness of another person because every aspect of the relationship is determined by the contamination of previous experience. Failed trust, personal attack, and personal hurt have happened so often at vulnerable and sensitive times that the pain of the past dominates. Everyone is seen as a potential or real assailant, someone who will painfully lead his or her victim into disappointment and betrayal.

The opposite extreme is the naïve and overtrusting person, someone with a simple worldview that doesn't allow for chicanery and deception. These people get into problems with psychopaths and other life liars. They are unable to see the complexity of people and unable to make a clear judgment of their good and bad qualities. They do not have the reasonable suspicion of a fully developed adult.

The healthy perspective is to see all others as complex beings capable of good and bad behavior. A person earns trust by being trustworthy; he or she does not automatically have trust as a personality feature. Relationships over time delineate this quite well to the observing person. Trust, like many values in life, is another asymptote. It is something strived for, never total.

We can overestimate or underestimate the ability of another to be trustworthy. Youngsters are prone to overestimate trust when sexual matters are concerned. Here is an example from clinical practice:

A twenty-five-year-old feels betrayed by her boyfriend. He is the person with whom she had her first sexual experience. She knew him for years, beginning in high school. She had dreamed of marrying him. A few years ago he developed a drug problem and secretly stole thousands of dollars from the girl and her parents.

She feels perplexed at his behavior and cannot understand why he would hurt her after their long, loving relationship. She has severed the ties with him but continues to yearn for him. He promises to do better, has gone into rehabilitation, and swears he is in the process of stopping drugs. He declares his love for her. She is too angry to give him another chance but wonders whether she should or not.

The problem rests not in betrayal, but in the girl's not assessing the correct personality and style of behavior in the boy. He was troubled before he started drugs, and drugs became the manifestation of his unhappy home life. The girl should never have trusted him in the first place and should have based her expectations on his behavior, not on her idealization of her first love. She was blinded by the sexual issue, her own insecurities, and his professed dedication. Her parents had given her no equipment with which to judge this boy. She was especially vulnerable because the sexual element was so strong.

The issue of betrayal lays responsibility partly in the limited judgment abilities of the betrayed. Certainly, there are psychopaths and deceptive people, but most show their true nature after an extended time. It is only necessary to read the signs and be truthful to oneself. Explaining away bad behavior or getting caught in the inadequate explanations of the other person does not lead to a happy outcome. Trust becomes not only an expectation in another person, but an understanding developed by the assessing person. In trust issues, it is most important to read the signs when they are displayed, and they are always displayed.

FRIENDSHIPS

Friendships are essential in life. After parents, the marital partner, and children of one's own, friends take center stage. Those who avoid isolation and enjoy uniting in reverie do better. Religious groups are an important supplier of friends, and this is one of the most compelling reasons for many to support their churches, synagogues, or mosques.

The feeling of community and mutual support given by these institutions is a healthy life adaptation for most.

Friendships, like marriages, require adaptations between people. Friends are drawn to each other by mutual interests and a commonality of beliefs. Friendships require a steady input of supportive behaviors. Each person enjoys the belief that the other will be there in times of difficulty. "She has my back" is not an idle comment.

The degree of trust expected between two people is proportional to their tolerance for disappointment. No relationship is ideal, and all require compromise. This is certainly true of friends.

Accepting and indulging in a friendship demands a considerable degree of activity on behalf of one to the other. Neglected communication diminishes the bond, as does a failure to support one another. When invitations are given to a friend and the friend can't attend, explanations are necessary from the one receiving the invitation. Simply not showing up is a statement of insensitivity to the inviter. It should always be assumed that the inviter is sensitive to slights. All effort should be made to keep the air clear between two people.

It's important to remember again that people have their own histories and, therefore, their own problems. Many believe that friendship hinges only on the expressed behavior they observe; there is the feeling that the friend's history is irrelevant. This causes disruption in the bond when disruption can be avoided. The more that is known about the other person, the more that person's limitations and confused behaviors become understandable. We often need to forgive momentary indiscretions. This a requirement for a long friendship and should be the underlying maxim for a successful one.

Of course, it bears repeating that trust is the most important issue in a successful friendship. When a friend betrays that trust, the essential question is whether that betrayal is intrinsic to the person's personality, or whether the loss is a result of peculiar circumstances that probably will not be repeated. Every effort should be made to discuss the betrayal and understand the motivations beneath it. If the conclusion is that this is a personality trait that is likely to be repeated, the friendship has to be either dissolved or reduced in significance. It is important for the injured party to realized that the friend has a problem unrelated to the injured, one that does not allow for a strong, trusting, and dependable relationship. Reducing the frequency of contact is the easiest way to lower the intensity of the friendship. Ultimately, distance will dispel the bond.

Friendship is a crucial part of life. Since isolation is not healthy, every effort should be made to obtain and sustain friends. However, like all relationships, understanding psychology enters into its success. Every offense is not personal and designed to hurt. Appreciating the pressing issues in the other person's life is one of the crucial elements in maintaining any relationship. When the burden of continuing is greater than the benefit of stopping, the friendship has to be dissolved. This is always painful. The decision to break off is based on the realities of the expected benefit and the pain of repeated disappointments. Dissolving a friendship should never be interpreted as a personal failure. Any relationship lost is difficult, but holding on to a bond that is mostly hurtful is unnecessarily destructive to the self.

SUICIDE

Suicide is the atomic bomb of human relations. When people kill themselves, they are exploding a weapon that affects all who are nearby and many who are emotional distances away. Suicide is a communication. On the surface it appears the message is that despair and pain became too much for the self who inflicted death. Underneath, the message is usually rage at the surrounding world. The immediate recipients of the suicide message are the closest: brother, sister, mother, father, daughter, son, husband, lover, friend, or wife. These people are being attacked.

The suicide is a person who is in pain and has given up. The feeling is that there is no way to relieve pain or despair. Further, the suicide believes him- or herself alone and that no one is listening. This belief is often maintained in the face of a not appreciated different reality in which everyone wants to help. In family wars, the pain may consist of rage, and the suicide intends to communicate this rage in place of any verbal statement. The person committing suicide feels that words do not work; he or she believes some severe act is necessary. Even though the suicide victim will not be around to watch the recipients of the message suffer, the person imagines the reaction and gains pleasure as the last breath of life leaves his or her body. The nonchalant note of many suicides is most misleading. Most notes talk about the importance of not forgetting this or that, admonishing in advance any neglect of the refrigerator or the cat. The suicide note gives the illusion that the person truly expects to check on the survivor and that the survivor's *post mortem* behavior is important to him or her. Ultimately, it is the act that is the message, not the note.

Those who remain behind after the death are often wracked with guilt. They question how they might have saved the victim, how they misread the signals, how even a few moments in attendance or that neglected phone call might have made all the difference. The true problem is that the suicide wanted to communicate the difficulties in the relationship but could not, or perhaps the suicide never felt heard. Usually, a completed suicide is designed not to be discovered until it's too late. The successful death is planned so that the body is found by the right person at just the right time. All this is in the fantasy of the perpetrator.

In suicides that are forewarned, where people tell someone they are planning to kill themselves, the warning must always be taken seriously. The afflicted may make many attempts with no intent to actually die, yet death may be the result anyway; this "gesture" suicide can be just as dangerous as the carefully planned. In these cases, the message to the potential suicide should go something like this:

"Suicide is the atomic bomb of human relations. Everyone you know will be damaged by your act. There is no escaping. No one will see this as warranted no matter how much pain you are in. There is always an alternative, even though you don't see one at this time. Depression is the seedbed for suicide. If you have a depression, it should be treated. If you are considering killing yourself because of your anger at [insert name here], you would accomplish more by telling [insert name here] than killing yourself. Your death by your own hand will leave a legacy for your loved ones and your children. In your family, for generations to come, the idea of killing oneself to solve a problem will be established. Your death increases the likelihood that your children will consider that option. The guilt you engender in family and friends will cause incalculable harm to them. This harm goes beyond the value that your act will have for you."

If this rational argument does not work, the potential suicide should be hospitalized.

Close survivors of the successful suicide must be made aware of this terrible game the victim has played. The anger the survivor feels because he or she has been put in this undeserved position by the suicide should be elicited and assuaged as best as possible. The victim's despair, severe irrationality, and the feelings he or she had of being trapped can be illustrated to help the survivor adjust to the idea that one would have done any reasonable thing to help prevent the death. Survivors must be shown the irrational position of the suicide and helped to appreciate how they, the survivors, are being used. In death, the suicide victim inflicts on the close survivor a great deal of pain, attempting to make the loved one suffer in proportion to the suicide's death. Anything seems justified to demonstrate the suicide victim's pain. This is unfair and excessive. Suicide is an extreme act for which alternatives always exist. This is why the still-living feel the disproportion of the act. The unnecessary hurt was always part of the suicide's plan.

These are the issues in the majority of self-inflicted deaths. The exceptions include planned death in an atmosphere of euthanasia. For example, Sigmund Freud asked his physician to help him die when he was in the throes of pain from mouth cancer. Some have taken their lives when about to be captured by an enemy. Most suicides, however, follow the outline in the above discussion, and the act is usually one of rage designed to destroy or hurt others. These are frequently the unconscious thoughts; the suicides rarely think them through with a clear mind.

If rage is often the motivation, how do clinicians handle this with survivors? Clinicians often like to point out that suicide is the murder of two people. One is the victim him- or herself, and the other is the person or persons in the suicide's mind as he or she commits his or her act. Suicide for medical reasons can be premature and even inaccurate. Some choose a Kevorkian death while believing their illness is terminal, but medical knowledge could have demonstrated otherwise. Psychological factors play into their visit to the Death Doctor, and these factors are ignored by the enthusiast.

Suicide, then, is almost always an irrational act by a tormented person in the throes of a depression. The feelings and motivations are pathological and without supportable logic. It remains a symbolic murder in which the survivors share the victim role with the suicide. It is a terrible final behavior in the human arena and always leaves permanent scars for the immediate survivors and generations afterward.

THE INDIVIDUAL VERSUS SOCIETY

• • •

WE ALL LIVE IN AND around other people. Studies have shown that two or more people can significantly influence the thinking and choices of a single person. Most of us feel torn between our thoughts about life and the behavior and opinions of others; the certainties of the larger world are not always compatible with the person in it. Because we are all so immersed in our cultures, we do not see the borders between self and people at large. A group operates differently than a person. For example, in the Ray Bradbury story "Hate," a stadium of people cry out the word *hate* at someone in the center of the stadium field with such venom that the person dies on the spot. Though this illustration is a fictional extreme, it is a rare person who can withstand the opprobrium of a group.

Most people are uncertain regarding their abilities in the social context. For some, self-esteem and confidence are fragile aspects of who they are, and these people are more susceptible to the slings and arrows of life's difficulties. In the arts, for example, the uncertain student of music, painting, or performance is at the mercy of the teacher. Many a beginner has been deterred from something he or she loves or enjoys by a dominating, overidealizing teacher who insists the novice cannot learn the craft that is so important to him or her. The teacher, in this instance, often lacks empathy because of failed ambitions of his or her own. The teacher may come from a home or a learning experience in which he or she was severely criticized. Now the teacher unwittingly plays out his or her personal drama on the student.

Criticism, then, is a potent tool for the troubled teacher. When properly applied, criticism is the cornerstone of the education of the new learner; criticism can also be a detriment for development. All criticism must be interpreted in this context. The worst position a student can take is to accept criticism uncritically. Guidance comes from a human being, and this person has a history. In the best context, the teacher has the welfare of the student at heart and delivers all the criticism in a kind and thoughtful manner. Comments are truly meant to help, and teachers usually take the students' naiveté and ignorance into account. Stumbling is seen as a way station for growth, not an indicator of a singular inability to master the task.

The imperious teacher who feels like the gatekeeper for a particular goal is dangerous. Some beginners may not have the talent for an achievement and need to be advised. The novice has a right to be taught and not shoved to the side because a teacher deems him or her inadequate for the desired discipline in the future. However, this is very hard to determine in many cases. The bumbler of today can easily become the outstanding talent of tomorrow. Motivation often trumps original poor promise. Over a long period of time, the gatekeeper teacher can do serious harm. The new learner has no awareness of these psychological issues in a teacher and is therefore extremely vulnerable to the gatekeeper's condemnations.

Criticism, as with all ideas in language, deserves interpretation. It is almost always a psychological matter between two people. Their temperaments, their goals, their histories, and their personalities all play a role in what, ultimately, the criticism means. The student's talents, his or her individual psychological background, and his or her attitudes toward learning play a major part. Unfortunately, it is rarely the case that the student interprets criticism correctly. Many lives have been damaged by shallow and harsh comments against someone's performance. The kind, talented, and caring teacher who sees the development of the student as the primary goal is rare. Many teachers simply have not developed to that level of psychological appreciation and misplace the essence of their task. Though maintaining the high standard of performance is important, the future welfare of the student is more so. No one should be left destroyed by an overcritical teacher.

Finally, criticism is a difficult undertaking. There is no easy way to evaluate anyone since many ambiguities and uncertainties interfere. Even in the best hands, assessing someone correctly is a challenge, and there is always room for error. All evaluations should be undertaken with humility and a full awareness that the person evaluating might make a mistake. Though all of us have opinions of others, none of us is so accurate as to stand on our conclusions with full confidence. Evaluations, like everything else, are prone to misinterpretations. All interpretations are estimates, but hopefully they reach an asymptote where all truth rests.

PREJUDICE AND DIFFERENCE DISCRIMINATION

A person's belief that someone else is inferior because of his or her differences can have many causes. Growing up in a critical and condescending home where the inferiority of others is often dramatized is certainly a common one. Unresolved sibling rivalry in which a sibling is felt to be held in higher regard is another. Whatever the origin of prejudice, the underlying feature is an irrational attempt to find others inferior to the self.

The reality of the social world is that minor differences do not make for inferiority or superiority. A higher IQ in someone may be matched with a tendency toward emotional misjudgment. A sensitive and caring person may have only a modest intellect. A handy person capable of impressive dexterity may also have difficulty reading. The terms applied to these people, terms such as *inferior* and *superior*, are global, covering all aspects of people. As such, these terms can never be accurate. One may feel good using these global terms in statements such as, "I'm superior to her." Though this can be satisfying, the sentence has no meaning beyond self-aggrandizement. The uncertain individual who must shore up his or her sense of insecurity by finding others inferior is the core problem.

The gender battle, in which one sex explains that the other sex is inferior, is a good example of overgeneralization of meaning. Sex contains so many variables that it is impossible to determine the inferiority of another person just on the basis of gender. Certainly, men and women are different. Perhaps women tend toward motherliness and care, and men tend toward aggression. Yet a survey of the sexes will find outstanding examples of these qualities on either side of the gender bar. The historical need of males to place women in inferior positions is no evidence of the accuracy of such placement.

Male sensitivities may be served by condescending to women, and women may have historically enjoyed this societal style. The behavior reflects on nothing of substance, nor is it accurate. Women may have muscle weakness in comparison to males, but women also live longer and suffer stress better. The concepts of the inferiority of women and the superiority of men are simply self-serving. The gender that advocates such a position in the overall assessment of the other is taking a fallacious path.

Any inspection of the history of Western culture makes clear that prejudgment and discrimination is a common feature. Nowhere is this more painfully evident than in racial discrimination.

There is no race. The word has no meaning except as a vague summary explanation for differences in people. The African American is different from the white. This is not a racial difference; this is merely skin color. Race is a nineteenth-century word that overgeneralized genetic differences. Gene (DNA) variance determines body shape, organ behavior, and body response. Superior and inferior are social judgments with no clear, objective connection to races that are clearly not the same. Genes may make someone smarter or of a different color, but genes do not make someone superior or inferior. Genes are connected to human characteristics, but whether the result is inferior or superior depends on issues beyond the slavery movement. It depends on human bias based on human psychology. Issues having to do with genes is subtle, complicated, and separate from the problems created by black-white prejudice.

Perhaps this question is best expressed by one of the eminent biologists of the past fifty years, Ernst Mayr, in his book, *This Is Biology*:

> The division of modern humans into races and the biological status of these races have been controversial...In the days of slavery the comfortable view was widespread among whites that whites, blacks, and the mongoloid Asians were three different species. This view has been totally abandoned, but the number of human races recognized by different authors—ranging from five to well over fifty—suggests that arguments over the meaning of "race" have not been resolved.

> Typological thinking is never enlightening in the study of life, but it has been most vicious and deleterious in the consideration of human races. Modern molecular research has revealed that all so-called human races are very closely related to one another. Their differences are simply variables in the populations. They often differ from one another in mean values for various physical, mental, and behavioral characteristics, but there is wide overlap of their curves of variation. [When we go beyond appearance and consider the behavioral differences or the] psychological characteristics that really count, the role of genes is largely undetermined.[2]

2 Ernst Mayr, *This is Biology: The Science of the Living World* (Cambridge: Belknap/ Harvard Press, 1997), 244–245.

Race is a political word, a word emanating from a society in a particular zeitgeist. In the politics of stating another is inferior, race is merely an epithet that may mean Hottentots, Aborigines, blacks, and other terms that connote "primitive." These are words that have no meaning today. They are words of idle classification and self-serving needs. If you want to sell people and enslave them, you have to demean their status and make them inferior. If they are similar to you, putting a price on their heads becomes more difficult. If you want to fight a war, it's good to make your enemies into "Japs," "Chinks," or "Wops." Fighting a war against people like yourself in which you are killing souls like your soul is nearly impossible for most people. You cannot easily murder six million Jews if they are of the same status as the average German. Similarly, murdering three million Cambodians requires that the victims be enemies of the state, an inferior group without the willingness to abide by the regime of the time. Race and its accompanying prejudice is a means to hurt others. These ideas are almost always in the hands of leaders who are troubled and pathological.

To live the sensible life, it is imperative to recognize prejudice when it appears. Understanding the manifestation of prejudices of a person or group with predetermined attitudes—attitudes not inspected and understood—is crucial. Sensitivity to excessive terms such as *superiority* and *inferiority* is required. When speaking of a singular quality in a person, such words are appropriate. After all, Horowitz was a *superior* pianist. Rembrandt was a *superior* artist. These singular excellences do not allow the overcasting conclusion that Rembrandt was a superior *person*. That determination is too inclusive.

When judgment terms are used to abuse, they should be eschewed. The idea in the time of slavery that the black man was an inferior species closer to apes than white folk was clearly self-serving to the slave owner. Our antennae should be raised and tuned when we see others using such conclusions to hurt. The only way society can cohere and be sustained is with a respect for others, however much they may differ from ourselves. Abusing people undermines the social fabric, leading to a spirit that can cause social disintegration and strife.

There is, therefore, no inferior race. There is no general human characteristic that justifies considering someone worse than anyone else. The medical insistence on treating everyone with human dignity can well be ascribed to society at large. The racial discord of America's history, the slavery of Western history, and the genocide of global history are all to be remembered as examples of human folly. The need to make others inferior and, moreover, to kill them, is a pathology. There is no alternative way to view this. All efforts and all thoughts must be directed to discard racial discrimination thinking. Without a respect for others and their differences, the center of any society will not hold.

GOVERNMENT

If three or more people are placed together for the purpose of living together, they will form a government. One will be chosen as the leader or spokesperson for the other two. The group will make rules that the leader will enforce. This is a natural biological tendency in humans and in other less conscious animals (primates, wolves). Though in other animals, the leader may be chosen by strength demonstrated in battle, the so-called alpha male or alpha female, in humans other features may determine who will lead. Whatever the criteria, the group as a whole is better suited to survival if there is a government, so there is a strong inner imperative to forming one.

In any case, without even the concept of democracy, the small group government is based on the fact that the members of the group designate and accept the leader. He or she governs only so long as the others wish. The leadership position is lost when the members no longer want to abide by their original compact.

This natural inclination means that there will always be government. Anarchists may not like the government against which they protest and wish to destroy, but when the anarchists are dispersed, a government will reform. No society can exist without it.

Jefferson and others realized this in the creation of the United States. They also realized that the group (e.g., the people) was not always reasonable. Though the people chose who was to lead them, their choices often would prove problematic. Franklin, Jefferson, Madison, and others agreed that there must be protections to prevent the problems that come upon society when a bad leader is chosen.

Governments are best when they are there for the governed and worst when they are there for the government. A state that demands its people live for the state alone is a dictatorship. The individual is lost to the purpose of the laws; the laws are created merely to sustain the power in control.

So far in the Western world, governments have evolved for the people who are the law's subjects. Rulers exist to improve the lives of their constituencies. Laws allow for order and reasonable transactions in human affairs. There must be a sentiment to allow for this, a consensus in the population that determines governments will be contrived to serve the people under them. Without this sentiment, the society may be managed in a very different manner. Democracy is never automatic.

The first democracy, the Athenian democracy, was problematic. Only landowners and men could vote. What constituted these factions became complicated, but never did the individual become the prominent concern. It was an upside-down democracy in which Athens was to be served by the people, and the people might or might not be served by Athens. There were few checks and balances. Plutocrats and prejudice ruled. Thus was Socrates sent to death.

The American system is a great improvement over the Athenian. Often unappreciated by its own population, the United States is based on consensus battling special interests. The election system is complicated and only barely results in choices that are representative of the people's desires, yet the operation of government is mostly serviceable. Plutocracy continues to have its sway, and money remains a great overweening power; still the decisions of government are mostly pointed toward the constituents. The Western democracies are probably the most people-friendly in the history of the world.

Given the often misguided and downright wrong decisions of current governments in the West, what keeps the mechanism running? In short, the people are largely satisfied. They are not always satisfied, but they believe the rules of living together approach fairness. It is psychology that makes a government effective. As long as there is a spiritual concordance, and as long as the general population feels that the government is legitimate and more or less reasonable, the process of rule will continue.

Therefore, government is always fragile. It can dissolve quickly if the consensus is lost. This is not a matter of electoral consensus, but a matter of emotional (viz., spiritual) acceptance. The *vox populae* sounds out a "yea" or behaves implicitly with consent, and the government continues.

The difficulty of throwing over an operating dictatorship is considerable. How many people of Africa would like to rid themselves of murdering, irresponsible leaders? Guns will dominate. The individuals will try to gain an advantage, but the problem in overthrowing one tyrant is mostly in the hands of a group. Once the group wins, the problem of decent governance arises. A society without a tradition of fairness has a great difficulty forming a government that is responsible to its constituents. Even if the sentiment is there, the attitude toward new power is the crucial element. Without the proper social spirit, the government cannot work.

We are all forced to live with faulty governments. The question is how faulty? The degree of disappointment in the US system is considerable. There are even elements in society that want to disband the government altogether. These people have not thought the matter through. Forming an administration for the people that works for the good of all is a formidable task, and nihilism or anarchism becomes a cancerous attitude. Rather, every effort should be made to improve on the powers we have in place. There is no perfect government. Special interests, political factions, poorly constructed election rules, and simply incompetent officials make for poor governance. These problems will always exist, but we can work together to keep them to a minimum.

Government is important, though imperfect. No society can persist without one. From the family, the fundamental unit of government, to the presidency of the United States, there is no way to avoid the rule of others upon us. As long as the current dominant power respects the law and the law applies to all, the rule of the moment is satisfying. Time and again, countries without a strong rule of law have eaten away at their people until their own systems are destroyed. Those nations with a rule of law do better. The Western world is rich and strong because of this rule of fair-minded law. One wonders why everyone hasn't learned this.

The sensible life confers upon the government its due but remains suspicious of it. Sensible people make every effort to support reasonable laws, knowing all the while that all laws are not reasonable. Faith in the establishment is not a good idea, and proportional skepticism is warranted. Cooperation for the most part is adaptive, and one should express civil disobedience only in the most extreme conditions. A hostile attitude toward laws and government is not in the best interest of life. While government is always imperfect, if it mostly serves the people, its citizens may tolerate it. Plutocracy cannot be abolished, but it can be contained.

RELIGION

There is no God. There is no specific god.

There is a Brahmin god, Shiva; a Jewish god, Yahweh; an Islam god, Allah; a Mayan god, Kulkukan; a Greek god or gods, Zeus and Apollo and Diana, but no overriding, titular God. How can there be a singular force? After all, each god has a different configuration and a different description. When people ask, "Is there a god?" they are asking a poorly formed question; everyone with a god answers with a different entity in mind. The biblical god has even changed over the past two thousand years. In the beginning, this god was a harsh, critical male god rarely satisfied with his "chosen people." In book two, he became the god of Christ, a merciful power acting through his only son and caring about the weak and enslaved. Since humanity defines its honorific of God with so many different characteristics, the question about God gets confusing. Is humankind supposed to choose a god among the many offered? Is humanity trying to decide the basic question about whether there is a god?

First, is there a god, any kind of god?

Second, what is the god like, and which group of people does he or she claim? Is he or she associated with anyone? Are the people of a special god special, or just biased?

I realize that the questions multiply. As you think about it, the question of God becomes the question of people. What is it about people that make them have gods, see those entities so differently, and persist in believing that their vision is the correct one? This question can easily become an anthropological one. Do people need God, did people invent God, and does he or she exist outside of people and their ideas at all?

You can see where this is going. If God is at the apex of religion, why religion?

Why religion? Why God?

A serious problem we get into whenever we sincerely discuss these matters is stepping on somebody's toes. Is it possible to discuss these issues without offending anyone? I think not. The God believer and the religious person tend to dislike anyone who suggests that the foundation of his or her philosophy about existence is in question. Yes, being religious is the same as having a fundamental philosophy about life. In effect, you answer the long-standing question of "Why am I here?" while refusing to conclude "I don't know" and leave it at that. This gives you a fierce point of view and a decisive position that you know the truth about your existence and you will agree only with like-minded people who hold to the same truth.

At first blush it would seem the atheist answers the question, but this is misleading. The atheist is convinced there is no God. He or she has concluded that the position he or she prefers is that of an *a-theist*: a person without God. He or she jumps from this to saying there is no God—an arrogant position. The agnostic answers that he or she doesn't really know if there is one or not, but he or she cannot believe in the Old Testament idea. Neither the atheist nor the agnostic deals with the question of the ambiguity of the language of God. So when the atheist or agnostic avers his or her position on God, the nonbeliever is inadvertently referring to the biblical god and, usually, taking a position that the standard-issue God is not in his or her belief system. I wonder if many of these two "absolute" nonbeliever types would be able to describe the nature of the god they deny. Most often, they are merely attacking the established cultural description of God and condemning the social prejudice of God's existence.

Let's then look at whether there could be any god from any faith? Of course there could be, but what would such a concept be? Suddenly we see that any structured concept of God comes from the culture that describes it. The idea of God becomes a linguistic—or semantic, if you prefer—construction that is hardly understandable between *Homo sapiens sapiens*. Language becomes the barrier to the resolution of the God question. Without the believer, the atheist, the agnostic, or even the philosopher realizing this, the question of God becomes nothing more than a social entanglement.

Having acknowledged this, the God question remains, and the answer is most unsatisfying. We simply do not know if there is a god of any kind who governs the universe in which we find ourselves. We cannot even be sure if the question is constructed correctly because it has in it the presumption that we are looking for a *Homo sapiens sapiens*–like being who (or that) is in charge of us and everything around us.

Central to this discussion is why we humans even investigate these possibilities. There seems something in us that requires an answer, and all the answers come under the heading of religion with a capital *R*. Like it or not, atheist or not, it is impossible not to recognize the importance of religion. Religion is everywhere. There is no known culture that does not have an explanation for life couched in religious terms. With religion being so universal among humanity, and with so many different interpretations of "our reason for being" and the "meaning of life and death," it behooves us not to dismiss religion lightly.

Most often you hear atheists or agnostics decrying religious people, leaving themselves in a state of overweening confidence, a kind of supercilious sense of the naiveté of others. In fact, this becomes a foolish position. When surveying our fellow humans, we find the vast majority of them are religious to some extent. It would be folly to dismiss such an important and widespread human concern.

The question of the existence of God and the system of religion in which this question always resides is clearly of great importance to humans. Whether nor not Marx was right about religion being an opiate to the masses, religion is a way of life. Is it any wonder that many hold to their beliefs tenaciously as a guide for daily needs?

If the inconsistencies of various religions stand out, this does not belie the importance of religious beliefs themselves. Humans need religion, and anyone who says otherwise is a poor anthropologist, to say the least.

This leads us to two positions: those who take a stand on religion and say they are religious versus those who remain outside of religion. Where you find yourself in this debate depends somewhat on your ability to accept a figure of human character who knows all and guides all. This massive assumption is made by the vast majority of humans on this earth. Why?

"If it walks like a duck..." In other words, people need religion, and they almost always put a parental figure in the center of it. The Catholic Church enjoys referring to its parishioners as children or "flock." God becomes the father of these children. Zeus was the father of the Greeks (after he killed his father, Chronos, who was going to kill him). Osiris was the father of Egyptians. Brahmins are the fathers of the Hindi. You can't escape the parental figure, and even a cursory view of any faith reveals one in it somewhere. Jesus may have come to earth to relieve the sins of humanity, but his mother, the immaculate Mary, is deified by much of the world as the mother of God. The message is that religion exists because none of us can escape our childhoods. We were brought into the world and lorded over by huge, tall, controlling parents for a long time. We are inclined to want to see the universe in the same way. There has to be a parent out there who will take care of us, make sense of it all, and be eternal so we won't die. The alternative is nearly impossible to accept. If there is no parent, no God, and no explanation beyond individualized religious interpretation, what is there?

The answer is either the cosmos, or no explanation. Let's look at each.

Humans search the cosmos, space, solar systems of planets, galaxies, and other planets for answers regarding origins. The explanation comes in the form of star explosions creating and combining chemicals that made earth and earth-like planets, which gave rise to life. This process occurred over tens of billions of years, while our developing earth took a little more than four billion of these. SETI (Search for Extraterrestrial

Intelligence Institute) is designed ultimately to reassure us that there are other earths far away in this cosmos. These earths have beings that think like us. What caused the universe, the explosions, the combinatorial possibilities? There is a big question mark on that one. Those who adhere to this perspective live with the question mark. Their religion becomes the unknown. They are stuck with the mystery. Like Br'er Rabbit in "The Tar Baby," they are implanted firmly in the tar of uncertainty, and they make their peace with it. Life, for them, becomes unknown, unexplainable, and acceptable as a mystery. "I don't know" becomes the mantra. These people encourage science and take part in the search for the answer, but they suspect that God will not be the explanation. Stanley Kubrick notwithstanding, those of this position will never see megaliths in space or symbolic newborns circulating around a planetary system.

There is no shame in refusing to live with severe uncertainty, always in a state of searching for a better explanation than the one at hand. However, all humanity is in the same existential boat. Whether they are people immersed in the mystery of uncertainty or people entrenched in the comforting idea of a parental God, all will live their days on this planet, die, and be dissipated into this earth's soil. Their beliefs will die with them, except for those thoughts transmitted by memes to those who listen to their teachings and incorporate them into their lives.

So the world is divided into two masses of people. By this reckoning, one unit is a small mass of mystery lovers who eschew any explanation, including a parental God, and the other is a massive group (almost everybody) who believes in one form of parental god or another. Can they get along?

Within this self-protective embrace of religious conviction is the sense that absolute adherence is required. Those of religious faith promulgate the certainty that without absolute adherence, their entire edifice will fall apart. These prayers must be said, these acts must be performed, and these "others" must be eliminated if the power of the given religion is to be kept. Without this insistence and the promise of immortality, all of the attractions most religions hold will disintegrate. This testament to the unique quality and desperate need of the religion in question creates social problems and is the source of most religious conflict. This is religion beyond philosophy, beyond a way of life, but religion as a banner cry for holding one people superior to another.

Religion is not of itself a bad thing. Besides a belief system that gives comfort to those who see life as a threat toward annihilation, it is also a powerful social structure. Religion keeps people together; it fosters social cohesion. It becomes a form through which the uncertain life can be lived. Religion and tradition are closely joined. Religion was invoked as much to keep the tribe together as it was invoked to give an explanation to existence itself.

Beneath and behind all this is the specter of death, that ghost who knows no one but the victims in life. In order to fully appreciate religion, it is necessary to look at this male in a gray-black mantle holding a scythe with a skeletal hand.

DEATH AND RELIGION
We all die.

We know this, but find it very troubling. The more valuable and satisfying a life is, the more difficult it is to acknowledge death. The physicists tell us that death is a part of a fundamental aspect of the universe: entropy. Entropy is the disappearing of organized energy, the loss of that activating process that drives life, planets, suns, galaxies, and even the universe itself. This may be true, but it doesn't comfort us to know that mortality is merely a part of the physics of everything.

Humans are the only life-forms who know death is ineluctable. No chimp foresees extinction in the life plan. Humans know all too well that they live a terminal existence. They don't like it and take all kinds of measures to avoid it. Besides cryogenics, diets, exercise, vitamins, and many other "solutions" to death, humans turn to religion. The chimpanzees, the bonobos, the orangutans, and the gorillas do not know about death. This is not a certainty, but although a chimp may run from a danger, tear apart a small monkey for food, or be fearful in front of an alpha male, there is no evidence that any of this includes a conscious awareness of death. Though we may see a television documentary in which an elephant mother nudges the lifeless body of her dead child before walking away, this doesn't translate into the elephant's contemplation of this event. It isn't death that the elephant or the chimp understands; it's the lifeless body. The body's remains does not mean "death" in the verbal, connotative way we appreciate the meaning of death; it means that the corpus of the once living elephant is lifeless, not present. The transformative significance of the dead animal is absent to all investigation in the surviving elephant's thinking. (We don't really know what "thinking" means in elephant terms.) Is a memory of the once living friend persistent, or does the now absent living friend or child only signify the body is absent of life? We can't be sure, but all studies on other animals suggest that the concept of death as we know it is probably different. The elephant cannot anticipate what has happened as we do. The massive creature can only register the absence of life. The abstraction of anticipated death is unique to humans; therefore, only humans contemplate their own demise.

What do we do with this awareness? We invent solutions, and the greatest solution is religion. Some may see this conclusion as a cynical position designed to denigrate religion. The truth is completely the opposite. Religion is a great institution that allows large-brained mammals to live despite their knowledge of death. The problem arises when the solutions offered by religion are viewed as beyond the human condition, an explanation devoted to miracles.

The human mind has the ability to enter trance states. This can be done with or without drugs. The word *trance* is difficult to define, but it can be viewed as a state of mental being in which the internal sense is predominant while the external world seems to disappear. For some with religious fervor, the trance becomes the means to experience a "higher power." These religious experiences were first clearly described by William James in *The Varieties of Religious Experience.* In his work, he makes the point that the convictions arising from these meetings with the deific are intense. He adds that body changes, rashes, pseudoseizures, shaking, babbling as if speaking a foreign tongue, sweating, and vomiting can all result from a tranced state.

With or without a trance, anyone may experience a special feeling of ecstasy (or simply pleasure) through art or meditation. All of this is part of the human experience. The moment of sensing this so-called religious world is no proof of God, gods, or spirits. Most ecstatics have lived a life seeking this kind of "miracle," but there is no miracle occurring. The brain can create dreams, ecstasy, trances, and out-of-body states and then imbue these experiences with a belief. Observed in the cold light of day, these religious conversions or sensations are the lifelong result of using the brain's natural abilities to solve a problem through religious feeling. This mundane explanation is probably the right one. Anyone can experience the "power of the Lord" if his or her mind is prone to do so. When it happens, it does not mean that the Lord is in him or her or that the Lord is experiencing that person. It does mean that the susceptible person is ascribing the Lord to the psychosomatic body reactions the belief and trance state have created.

Most Western religions are connected with the two Bibles, both of which deal extensively with resurrection—that is, non-death. These Bibles reassure believers that their mortal lives are merely a passage to an eternal one, a reassurance that defies all observation and scientific knowledge today. One of the underlying reasons for religious groups being intolerant of Darwinism and science in general is the tendency for these disciplines to deny the possibility of non-death. Magic, myths, and religion are overtly or covertly mired in the belief of life after death. Hostility toward science by creationists and fundamental religious believers is thereby easy to understand.

Imagining the extinguishing of the mind or soul (a word that has come to mean many things, including the entirety of what makes someone him- or herself) is a troubling and difficult task. The sense of life is so powerful that we are forced to avoid the fact it will terminate. The trouble with grasping onto the unlikely idea that life may be extended into an afterlife is that the notion defies all evidence and leads us into prejudices that distort reality. The Enlightenment and the diminishing of religious control over thought have brought benefits to humanity beyond any fifteenth-century expectation. The forces that opposed the Enlightenment feed ignorance, a lack of progress, and theocratic brain numbing. The conclusion has to be that adherence to testable ideas is superior to belief in untestable myths. Checking the foundations of convictions is beneficial. Adherence to convictions in the face of contrary evidence is socially destructive.

This leaves us with the overwhelming evidence that death is inevitable, and we must make our peace with this. The task is in no way easy. Realizing that we will be eliminated from the world we know, that history will be played on without us, and that our influence over our loved ones will be extinguished are all torments that must be accepted. The belief that we can both affect the living now and leave a legacy through creative efforts helps to mitigate the pain of death.

The funeral is unwittingly designed to emphasize the importance of legacy and effect. The dead cannot hear what is said, so speeches about the dead are meant for the living. The good qualities that form the basis of the eulogy are communications to the living audience that they should also possess these qualities. Funerals, while helping us deal with the loss of loved ones, are also an inspiration that we should live with the values of the deceased and that our continuation is meaningful.

The ritual in which we say good-bye to the deceased reinforces most living beliefs. Whether it's Valhalla or heaven, the congregation wants to be reassured that life continues in some form in some place. In Hinduism you may be reincarnated as a beetle, but you are reincarnated. No one is unimportant. Death itself shall have no dominion.

This is difficult to reconcile with the scientific estimates that the sun will die in some four billion years. The sun is a nuclear energy machine. Energy follows thermodynamic laws, and these contain the fact of entropy, a law of physics that shows all energy systems lose eventually. The sun will lose its ability to energize the earth; it will shrink first, then expand, and probably explode. At that time, all information, all lives, and all mortal creations will dissipate. Molecules will be released into space, but none will maintain their current form. History will be totally annihilated. Not only will all graves, all earth, and all religions be destroyed, but so will the memories associated with them.

There is, then, the individual's death and the death of the entire world connected with that person. If heaven, Valhalla, or the reincarnated person is a truth, these places will have to be somewhere besides earth. Earth will be gone.

For the living, this somewhere can only be one of two places. Either humans will succeed in their efforts to travel to distant planets and populate viable alternatives to earth, or ultimately the living will die and go to the imagined special places religion offers. In any case, the living are to experience a terminal event in the near future and have to make peace with themselves as best they can.

Whether you choose religion or the acceptance of the mystery, you still ultimately die. Living life with death hanging like the scimitar of Damocles is not always easy, and recommending the acceptance of death is not a position one can take with sanguinity. Religion, relationships, family, strong interests, and satisfying days all assist in this process. Isolation, misanthropy, and limited interests make the Grim Reaper appear almost as a welcome beckoning. Death should not cast a shadow over our daily lives, but it does. One must work to keep the shadow small.

PART 2

A VIEW OF THE WORLD

• • •

REALITY

"A TREE FALLS IN THE deserted wood. Is there sound?"

"What is the sound of one hand clapping?"

Why is Magritte's painting of a pipe inscribed, "This is not a pipe"?

These and many more puzzles of a like kind are based on one thing only—language. In the first, the idea is that "sound" can be viewed as a human experience. Does it occur without humans? Most would say, "Of course!" Others might ponder the thought that since "sound" is a human language word, without the human presence to register its meaning, it's not a realized item, existing in isolation or not.

Science may provide an explanation of phenomena that routinely operate outside of human involvement. Let's look for a moment at Newton's equation for the abstract effect of the gravitational field, that "force" that affected the apple's fall. After all, $F=ma/d^2$ x G operates whether a human is there to explain it or not. The fact that the equation is Newton's brain child and was altered by Einstein in certain conditions might temper enthusiasm. After all, the equation was invented by a man struggling with the way things fall on earth or what keeps planets in their orbits. Einstein invented modifications of the equation for things traveling near the speed of light. Both are human mathematicians. Mathematics is based on language. Language is used to describe the world as experienced by man. Gravity is a word, a linguistic pill to the illness of confusion over what makes apples fall. The word is not a replacement for the "thing" of gravity, something we are yet to fully comprehend. The certainty that comes from Newton's predictive mathematics is still a remote reality, something measured by its effects but in no way described beyond this. Language explains nothing; it merely comforts us with a mathematical formula. Confidence that the word equals the denotative entity is misplaced. We remain mostly confused by gravity even though we understand a great deal of its mathematics couched in words. Its reality eludes us still.

Certainly the second statement, "What is the sound of one hand clapping?" a koan for Zen Buddhists, is redolent with language twists. Sound? Clapping? One hand? What? All these words bury us in the mire of language meaning.

Magritte's painting of a pipe is a play on the foibles of language and human perception. It is a *painting* of a pipe, not an actual pipe. A viewer has to be a human with language to understand the joke. *Pipe* is a word, a product of the human brain. The word has no meaning outside of the human brain that created the word *pipe* from social interaction learning. This teaches that a word can be used in numerous ways. The syntax makes *pipe* a noun, but it is possible to use it as another form of speech. "Let's pipe down to the market" is a valid sentence. Words have meaning *only* in human context. A word in the middle of the woods with no one around has no meaning, let alone sound.

There is an inherent paradox in epistemology: we seek for meaning, but we must do it with meaning. Meaning is language. Language is human. Humans are doing the seeking. Paradox. It is an ouroboros, a snake gobbling itself via its tail. We are all ouroboroses of a kind. In the quest for understanding the world around us, we construct language and fool ourselves into thinking this conceptual world is somehow independent of our construction. "'Twas brillig, and the slithy toves" [3]seems meaningful for humans because it has prosody and syntax. Most humans delight in the phrasing's nonsense sense. However, until Lewis Carroll, there was no one who would have come up with this verse line. When it comes to understanding reality, human brain construction is all there is.

Of course I rest on the shoulders of Wittgenstein who describes this in his *Tractatus Logico-Philosophicus* (1921), a seventy-page book saying what I said, essentially, in the paragraph above. These ideas defy the

---

3 Louis Carroll, "Jabberwocky," in Through the Looking-Glass and What Alice Found There, 1871

notion that all meaning can be placed in logical symbols, as Bertram Russell and Alfred North Whitehead attempted to do. Ironically, Russell sponsored Wittgenstein at Cambridge. There lies another paradox. Russell and Whitehead tried to come up with a logic-tight, symbolic way of communication that eschewed ambiguity. They developed symbols such as the equal sign and the sideways *U* to indicate thinking transformations. If-then structures are one example of this. This approach belies Wittgenstein's, which posits that even the meaning of symbolic logic depends on human assumptions. No one can escape the tautology: language is conscious human brain and conscious human brain is language.

The profundity of this cannot be exaggerated. Even Kant argued for the *a priori* brain, which has built-in abilities to "understand" the world outside. Language ability is certainly one of these built-in items. For the past one hundred thousand years, the brain has been specifically designed to use language if the parental stimulus is there for it. If man is not the measure of all things, language is all that mental man is. Language cannot be measured because the measuring of it requires language. We are at a quantum-like paradox. What is impressive about this paradox is that so few seem to appreciate how powerfully it corrupts the understanding of the world.

Take the example of perception. The archivist will cite Bishop Berkeley and the idea that the perception of reality is always a brain construction. He then will deny that the church steeple exists at a distance because the brain is always reconstructing it in "the mind's eye" as he gets closer and closer to it. The sophist can then argue there is no church steeple, only the mind's idea of a church steeple; Magritte has this in his thoughts and paintings as well. The problem comes with the realization that Berkeley's argument requires brain language. All the words necessary to make the argument belie the argument. Wittgenstein's maxim that "if it's not a picture, it's nothing" also falls under the weight of language. A picture must be described, and the belief that the description is an approximation is dependent entirely on the acceptance of the language as merely the product of human manipulation.

When an elderly person becomes demented or a brain is damaged, language is modified and no longer gives even an almost accurate "picture" of the world. That is, the world now described is a distorted world created by the deficits of the brain operating with whatever remaining healthy brain is left. The confabulation, so routinely recognized by doctors, is a case in point. The patient lying in the hospital bed speaks of being in school, at work, in a camp, or wherever the brain takes him or her. When the doctor points out that he or she is lying in a hospital bed, that there is an IV pole next to the bed, and that the uniformed people around the bed are hospital staff, the patient is incredulous. The words have no meaning other than to confound the patient's conviction. To think clearly, you need an intact brain, and the intact brain thinks only with language.

As I write this, I'm hoping you appreciate and understand what I'm saying, but I realize that despite the high probability that you will, it is not necessarily the case that you will. This "defect" in communication is unavoidable. Norbert Weiner in *Cybernetics-The Control and Communication in the Animal and the Machine* (1961) showed that energy is never 100 percent efficient. All communication is energy bound; therefore, there is loss in all communication. The conceptual equation $I = M/N$ is translated as Information = Message divided by Noise. Noise is the necessary loss in all information transmission, or Entropy; and Message is the meaning gleaned from Information transmitted. The game telephone, which children play to their delight around a circle of message givers, is a simple illustration of this. In our digital age where zeros and ones create entire worlds of human meaning, it is not difficult to see energy loss as a noise of miscommunications. Lose a few zeros or ones, and the message is gone.

What I have discussed in this chapter is merely a utilization of what thinkers and scientists have been writing about for years. Surprisingly, the depth of the significance of these ideas continue to elude intellectuals. Philosophers write about qualia-driven perceptions, struggling to substitute the word *qualia* for the linguistic idea of knowing from a quality in the mind. They are making confusion without clarification. *Qualia* is a word and can have any meaning you want it to have. Problems arise from an invented and ambiguous word that alludes to the sense that the mind has of the world outside the body. The same thing happens with "synthetic" versus "analytic" concepts of sentence construction. These inventions churn thought, create insights, and partly compose the fabric of understanding the philosophers so ardently think. Philosophers are creating this fabric of understanding. However, they are inventions fraught with the errors inherent in human communication.

These verbals are not to be decried. However, the verbals must be seen for what they are—words created by humans to help them understand themselves and the world. These words have all the freight that all words have. Words like *qualia, analytic,* and *synthetic* are examples of the language paradox. We cannot understand reality; we can only approximate it. Language is a requirement. It's the only mechanism available to humans for any form of comprehension. Like the brain, the words that come from it are vague, confusing, and uncertain. What is missing in almost all philosophical discourse is the humility required to appreciate the limitations of comprehension. The speed of light, argued by Einstein's cosmological equations, can never be exceeded; the brain, too, has limitations, and these limitations are words.

The anthropomorphic and, perhaps, biased view is that the brain is limited to its functions originating in the forest. The food gathering, defense, hunting, tribal obligations, and mating required on earth for early human development were well met with the brain. The brain sees far enough, appreciates human interaction enough, and accurately determines the contents of the world enough when the demands are within range. This same brain, completely adequate for its beginnings, is not up to the quandaries and uncertainties of the modern (or current) time. Perception is distorted by lenses, knowledge has limits, color is a variable between people, advanced mathematical thinking exceeds the brains of most people, and medical advances have made mating and food contain a completely different mental meaning than ever before. Scientific understanding has led to viewing mating as part of the evolutionary process. Food is both nutrition, the source of early demise, but no longer a mere means of sybaritic pleasure or immediate sustenance. The tool in the early days of *Homo sapiens sapiens* was language, and language is limiting, confining, distorting, and ambiguous. It was sufficient for our ancestors, but not for us.

There are numerous examples of how language confounds us. In quantum theory we have action at a distance (entanglement), and light that is either a particle or a wave. These differences cannot be reconciled. There is no language to describe the confusion they create. One can fall back on a joke by John Wheeler, a famous physicist: "If you understand quantum mechanics, then you are crazy." Even here, the word *understand* belies meaning.

Language also gives us a false sense of security. The daredevil behavior of youth in which sky diving, bungee jumping, and mountain climbing are viewed as safe is an example of how our brains create confidence without logical substance. Language has a similar seductive quality. Confidence in beliefs and facts is a way of living with certainty in an uncertain life. Language is used to enhance this confidence. In a world where nothing is assured, language deceives tell us that certainty is with us when it is not. There is no way to live when every comment and perception is connected to a severe lack of confidence. When fully appreciative of the ambiguity in all meaning, how do we manage? Fortunately, there is enough resilience and room for safety in error in experiences that trusting our understanding for most things becomes a satisfactory requirement. If we make every step with the feeling that we will stumble, we cannot walk. The overconfidence that language instills is mostly a requirement of sane living. Nevertheless, the reflective person should never be fooled. We live in a sea of uncertainty with an inefficient body. Nothing is for sure.

This sea of uncertainty becomes obvious when we go on vacation. When the hotel receptionist asks for our IDs and our credit cards, we are suddenly connected, coded, and verified. Yet we realize the receptionist knows nothing about us. She doesn't know what our houses look like, what our interests are, whether our marriages are good or not, or what our special skills are. In form of fact, we are adrift in a new land with limited boundaries. Our paper IDs are not our true IDs. They are simply a minimal requirement for staying at the hotel, as are our passports to enter a foreign country. Our identities are lost to all but ourselves as we travel the world. We could be anyone. Actual reality, the reality of our identities, is dependent on personal agreements, accepted social boundaries, and information not yet shared. Our personal realities, therefore, are always limited and self-assuring, an illusion of meaning in a world where meaning depends on social knowledge of who we are endorsed by others.

Similarly, after the blue earth was seen from the moon for the first time, all of us became dramatically impressed with the limit of our boundaries and their extreme importance. Earth boundaries are our sense of the beginning and end of things. For centuries these boundaries consisted of national borders, beaches at the edge of seas, or the seemingly limitless sky. Suddenly, these limits of geography were exposed as not enough. Suddenly, the region beyond the sky required boundaries, and perhaps there were none.

This was not the first time humans knew there was an elsewhere, but it was the first time the full meaning of earth became imprinted on our minds. We know our addresses, our names, our domestic earth, and our domains of activity. All of this gives us a sense of "reality," a sense of identity, and a sense of who we are. Without these inner mental pieces of connection, we would be lost. In space there is no up, down, right, or left unless we contrive directionals to give us these feelings. "Up" is the North Pole, "down" is to the south. East is to the lifted right hand when we're looking northward, and west is to the left hand. This is all manufactured by us and has no meaning beyond us.

There is a general lack of appreciation of how much of understanding in life is made up by humanity to create a sense of confidence, a sense of boundaries. Even without considering the language conundrum, orientation is a created myth essential to our survival.

Not only are we not the center of the universe, but we are merely a part of a diverse and wildly scattered set of properties we desperately try to organize using our language facilities. Everything about reality is dependent on this.

Artificial intelligence, or AI, has a field day with declaring the brain is merely a computer. These enthusiasts enjoy showing how brain circuits are similar to electrical circuits and may operate with zeros and ones just like a computer, or they argue that a computer with zeros and ones can mimic a brain. Whether the output of a computer or a brain can ultimately be similar undermines what we know about how the brain works. No neuron is like an electric wire, though current is transmitted. The synapse or connection between neurons depends on organic molecular interactions completely unlike that of a circuit. The energy system of the nerve cell depends on ATP (adenosine triphosphate) and proteins. No computer yet has anything like this. The receiving nerve synapse is a complex living thing that contains numerous proteins receptive to a given set of chemical messengers. In brief, the brain has billions of these entities with no simple zero-and-one factor. The brain seems both analog and digital. The mechanism of brain operation remains to be unraveled in research. However, AI latched onto the word *circuit* and ran with it even though the word does not even get close to explaining what is going on in the brain. The melding of words such as *computer* and *brain* is inhibiting, preventing a real understanding of those structures. Most brain researchers ignore this AI zeal and focus on how the brain works. This question alone demands many lifetimes of knowledge not yet available.

So reality, like truth (a word), is an asymptote. The line we term *truth* treads its way toward meaning but never intersects the line of meaning in the world. There may be a sound in the woods or a table in the room, but both are experiences translated by language and the perceptual apparatus of our bodies. Truth or reality derives from words with which we struggle for sense and significance. We use words to make an understanding of words, knowing all the while the result is limited by the words themselves. Culture and its members have created an impressive world so far with these limitations. One can only be in awe of what has been accomplished with limited brains even more limited by language. We humans watching all this can only feel astonishment at the technological creations that affect our lives, for better or worse.

Philosophically, however, we are handicapped. The importance of realizing this cannot be overstated. Every thought, every utterance, every conceptualization of a point on a chart, and every discourse on meaning is affected by language. We're stuck in uncertainty and ambiguity. We must face it.

What this means is that there is no confidence. Perception is distorted by visual limitations, cognitive limitations, and knowledge limitations. Knowledge is limited by language. Certainty is a holy grail that doesn't exist, and living in this haze of interpretations in everyday life is limiting.

The world outside our brains is more complex and elusive than most can appreciate, as evidenced by members of the animal kingdom that sense a reality different from our own. The bumble bee sees petal colors we can't see. The elephant hears low-frequency sounds we cannot hear. The pigeon flies with magnetic detectors responding to the world's magnetic field that we can't detect. The reptile's tongue senses heat and odors that we can't sense. We adapt to the world in ignorance because we are only able to adapt within the confines of our needs. We rarely know what we're missing, but we're always missing a great deal.

The exotic nature of our environment is even more extreme. Our environment includes the organs of our bodies. The spleen, liver, heart, lungs, bowel, kidneys, and brain are all organs of life. These organs are made up of cells, living beings with an incredible complexity. All of these cells have intricate, energy-producing systems, chemical messenger systems, and life-sustaining metabolisms. We experience none of this, but they persist each day we wake up. Our bodies are colonies of organs functioning cooperatively to keep the whole unit alive. When we think of ourselves, we think of an entire being. We exclude from our minds that we are actually multiple beings working together. We use the word *self* as if it's controlled by the brain, and we are the brain. This is far from what's happening. The heart beats, the liver processes a bewildering assortment of chemical reactions, the absorptive surface of the gut allows for essential food chemicals to support the whole. All of this and more constitutes the self. The self that we ascribe to for comfort is the end-stage cognitive presumption of all these elements working. Our brains deny us this reality unless we investigate the inside as we finally have. The brain, then, creates an illusion of body singularity and integrity. Our views of the world, the reality around us, and the reality inside of us is a surface, momentary understanding, a shallow interpretation of this complex biological process that makes us who we are.

There is a world outside and a world inside our bodies. We can interpret only a part of it in both of these spheres of interest, and this interpretation is based on limited language. Words are applied to our experiences, and these words suggest interpretations of how we understand things. At best, our interpretations are close enough to sensory experience and the actuality of these worlds outside so that we don't run into too much trouble. At worst, we are led to an unjustified hubris that corrupts our humility and creates massive misunderstandings.

We *Homo sapiens sapiens* are a part, an element of the planetary systems, living and nonliving. Our brains deceive us into believing we are more separate than we are, and this deception contributes to war and misjudgments about our planet. All knowledge is faulty and language biased. All "truth" is an asymptote, an approach to the integrated "reality" of our worlds. The idea that there is a United States and an outside, non-United States is part of the Great Deception. Nationalism deceives. It a useful tool to defend territory and to inspire an army to fight for the homeland, but it is not an accurate way to feel about our place in the larger world. Always there is the earth, the world, and we are a part of that world. How we choose to understand the integrated wholeness of it and how much arrogance we show in being convinced of this understanding works as part of the history of the planet. Arrogance can lead to maladaptation, unnecessary wars, and even planetary destruction. Humility of our place is more likely to encourage peaceful arrangements between disparate peoples. We must keep in mind that we are always merely part of a larger whole. We cannot know everything; we cannot completely know anything—we can only strive toward understanding as much as possible, keeping in mind our *a priori* limitations in our brains and their perceptual gift of language.

Certainly humankind has done and learned remarkable things about the internal and external worlds. Who does not marvel at the technological history of humanity on this planet? There is no gainsaying that people are an amazing species, a species that "amazes" itself. We can also see the dazzle that makes us impressed by ourselves in the meanderings of a slime mold and the intricate maneuverings of ions across a brain synapse. Nature is startling in its innovations and complexity. We are not unique to nature, but a part of it. This is where the humility begins, and this humility is a requirement for the future of the human race. Humans are not the measure of all things, and they are not an island; humans are the thing being measured and are always part of the mainland, never alone. As he or she measures, he or she is measuring not only the outside of self but the self itself. The self is both the measurer and the measured.

This is the ultimate profundity of the metaphor in Heisenberg's Uncertainty Principle, first applied only to quantum mechanics. This idea is not only applicable to the not-so-simple electron, regarding its position and speed, but of important and apt significance when investigating the human being. We learn and we learn well, but all learning becomes an approximation, an appositive to our brain limitations. Like the instrument affecting the detecting of the physical electron, we are the instrument affecting and being affected as we study our world. Reality is an interpretation, never an entity unto itself. That is the reality of our mortal coil and the reality of the world in which it resides.

The question about what is real in any given circumstance becomes an approximation. The koan questions require a reduction in comprehension of the meaning of words. The questions taken literally cannot be answered. Taken in the context of Zen education, there is connotative significance. A Zen master teaches by the ambiguity of the question. The question in the culture of Buddhism is not meant to be answered.

Agreement on perception demands humility between people, although understanding is always a stretch, an approximation two agree upon in the morass of uncertainties. No absolute guidelines exist. Dictionaries are arbitrary, their definitions conceived by disagreeing people forced to compromise. Likewise, laws are language approximations of physical reality. Referring again to our gravity example, struggling to understand gravity is a struggle to find words that closely approximate the way gravity operates. A force field is a linguistic invention that demands consistency of meaning to be sustained as a concept. Science, the prevailing intellectual discipline of the moment, is itself a conception; its practitioners adhere to a set of explanatory facts as long as language is consistent, and the facts are not contradicted by new language.

Ultimately, explaining anything in life is a language game and a very serious one. Applying words to phenomena, using words to describe things like entanglement, explaining complex ideas with words that approximate meaning, almost always leave us in a sea of uncertainty. Matters work out best if we participants acknowledge this to be the case. At least this approach in which we appreciate and admit to ambiguity enhances philosophical consistency.

SCIENCE

Living requires some kind of standard for finding reality with the language we have. There has to be a technique, a method that assures that the path is the right one, or at least one that doesn't lead to hurt or massive error. Science is that method. If we cannot fully appreciate reality because the internal and external worlds confound our brains, how are we to check ourselves and correct our errors? Science requires this attempt to know our "reality" to be a constant, never ending investigative process.

Science is not a belief. It is a method. We cannot believe in science as there is no final noun to which we can adhere. Science, though nominative, refers always to its very use and form. Science is discovering, holding temporarily to the best conclusions available, and then dismissing those conclusions when information contradicts the earlier consideration. The findings of science become "right" and then "wrong," and with new discoveries a new "right" emerges. Science is not some megalithic system of thought that denies religion. It is a method that asks religions to substantiate their conclusions or to change their beliefs. If you approach a religious person and say, "There is no God," he or she becomes irate and dismisses you. If you approach a person who uses science and say, "Your method is faulty," the likelihood is that such a person will say, "Show me."

Science is not perfect. The method is used by humans and is, therefore, subject to human error. Because the method is always correcting itself and always being reexamined, the truth—or reality—is approached. Without this technique, all statements become suppositions, beliefs, prejudices, and convictions. One person's conviction is no better than another's. No one can win an argument because evidence is unimportant. Evidence is all we have. It's quality is crucial and must be tested where possible, but throwing evidence away and stating that your conviction is the correct side of the discussion is untenable. Then, all that counts is self-confirming conviction. This is the mode of operation—evidence being shunted aside in place of faith—in most heated debates regarding religion.

Science is not perfection. No human enterprise can always guarantee success. Science can lead to lies. In more extreme cases, science in the mind of a fervent believer can lead to death. This is the point of Mary Shelley's *Frankenstein*. Frankenstein made assumptions, had beliefs, and operated blindly to create his monster because he wanted to defeat death. This novel is the method of science on a grand scale. Shelley was right to point out the dangers of the method run amok. Science should always be an information-gathering tool, never a means to wreak havoc because not enough information is available to hold back extravagant

and dangerous gestures of confidence. Good science is always the process of feeling insecure and cautious. A good Dr. Frankenstein, limited
by fear, would never have created the monster, but Dr. Frankenstein's
egomaniacal worldview led him to behave without science while he operated under the disguise of science. The real problem in Shelley's por-
trayal was not that of science; it was that of hubris and poor judgment.

Despite its failings, science is our best method and has led to wonders in our world. No other mode of thinking works as effectively and as
accurately. Even so, humility warrants that this truth be taken cautious-
ly. Just because something works better than all others does not mean it
can be trusted. No method can be trusted or accepted without criticism.
In *The Structure of Scientific Revolutions*, Thomas Kuhn shows science to
be a very human process that demands profound examination of itself.
Ideas such as phlogiston and celestial ether fell to the wayside because
of science, but at one time these ideas persisted because of stubborn human beliefs that fit these ideas to the answers required. However, they
simply were wrong. The ideas behind them could not stand up to experiment and scrutiny, so the concepts themselves were discarded.

Darwinism and quantum physics are also not beliefs. These disciplines are important because they describe the world to some extent,
but they are only worth adhering to until discoveries render their information untenable. Darwinism describes the worlds of speciation, studying why some groups of life are sustained despite the environment while
others disappear. This is not a belief like creationism. The creationists
are concerned with belief only. Facts outside of their one reference, the
Bible, are unimportant. Dinosaurs and humans coexisted because the
Bible suggests it, and geological records and fossil evidence mean nothing. They maintain their beliefs regardless of new, contradictory findings. Knowledge of anything is a struggle, a seeking out of accurate ideas.
If knowledge is an asymptote, a reaching for the nearly achievable, what
actually seems to be the proper conclusion is approached based on the

evidence available. Creationism is not knowledge. Adherence to any idea in the face of evidential material to the contrary is what keeps humanity in poorly maintained huts and with a conviction that eating neighbors enhances virility (as in New Guinea natives in the hinterland). Sooner or later, we must take a stand on some side of knowledge. Creationism is a stand that is counterproductive to civilization and human survivability.

So, like an Escher drawing of a hand drawing itself, science requires constant vigilance upon itself as a process. Its use is essential to live a life with meaning, but it is prone to error, to excessive enthusiasm, and to personal bias. Despite this, within the domain of the planetary world in which we live, there is nothing better. This way of thinking certainly has proved its value over the last three hundred years. The Ottoman Empire fell, in part, because it stopped all science. The Muslim religion was threatened in the fourteenth century by its scientists. Their labs and observatories were destroyed. Religious conviction was all that was tolerated. The Western world moved rapidly ahead because of this, and the Muslim threat was dissolved. With this in mind, just get into your automobile and drive somewhere. Without the scientific process, this would have been impossible.

ETHICS

Problems of morality are problems of language in the human arena. There is no ultimate or absolute right or wrong, only human opinions of right or wrong. Murder can be wrong. Murder can be right. The ultimate conclusion is nearly always social. Moral questions arise only in a social context.

Morality applies only to humans and does not exist in the animal world. The chimp may think taking the banana from another chimp is a value-laden activity. The chimp may behave as if the taking of the banana is superior over the leaving of the banana. His behavior deceives. He does not think he has done a superior thing. He behaves as if it is so but has no predictive concept that it is so. He does not see his behavior as "good" or "superior." He got the banana, and that's the end of his reflection on the matter. In brief, there is no mental language to illustrate the behavioral value. The morality of the chimp is behavioral only. This banana stealing may be value-laden to the observing human, but not to the chimp. Morality is human, and humans *invent* morality.

The subject of absolute morality often raises questions. Is there a right-wrong system that comes from the greatest power, the heavenly power, and the power of God? Many Christians will cite the highly ambiguous and inconsistent Bible as the source of absolute morality. The commandment "Thou shalt not kill" is merely one example. All the evidence suggests that the handing down of this commandment is not divine intervention; the statement is merely one of many adages in that great work of humankind. For those who want to believe in absolute moral dictums as indicated in the Bible, there is little more to be said. If you believe the Bible with all its ambiguities and inconsistencies, then that is your absolute. For those who wish to come closer to the nature of moral meaning, the quest for understanding must continue.

If we eschew absolute morality, and if we dispel the idea that there is some celestial or abstract rule for right and wrong that transcends human beings and human life, where does that lead us in comprehending right and wrong? How do we deal with the linguistic dilemmas that create moral paradoxes?

The train is coming. You can change the tracks so that the train kills one instead of five on another track. What do you do? This is a dilemma of human language created by humans. There is no solution because the conflict is designed by people to puzzle people. To some, "right" is defined by the number of deaths avoided, while to others, "right" is based on something else entirely. The morality of not killing is confounded by the puzzle. The solution is troubling because whether you kill one person or five, you are still killing. If anything, the question is more a message of the confusion of moral judgments than it is a genuine question. Since humans create the value "Thou shalt not kill," and the deific origin of such an idea is put aside, the problem rests in the nature of humanity. Humans try not to kill each other. You can contrive all manner of confusing and troubling dilemmas with such a value in place but not resolve the issue with a "correct" conclusion. There is no correct conclusion, only a human one.

This resolution, which seems unavoidable, is not necessarily unfortunate. Once you admit all morality is a human contrivance for social benefit, a kind of Benthamite[4] proposition, you are on the road to a consistency of ideas, if not a consistency of morality. Humans come from all manner of cultures, and those cultures dictate values. The values become the morality of the cultures. There is no natural reason why cultures should have the same moralities. If there is a commonality of values, it is because even people from widely different cultures are human. It's the homo sapient in them that makes for similarity, not some intrinsic system.

Some philosophers and religious leaders struggle to find the absolute in morality. There are those who use a logical and objective approach, hoping some universal human standard will emerge from different cultures. "Though shalt not kill" has often been held as an example. Religious leaders look for divine guidance through traditional religious texts. Many have touted the Golden Rule in its various forms: "Do unto others as you would have them do unto you." Even this admittedly fine adage cannot stand up to scrutiny as an absolute. Thinking beings all follow rules that help them complete boundaries of meaning in life. Though one can derive a universal rule from the human commonality

---

4 Jeremy Bentham was a nineteenth-century utopian who influenced the development in the town of Lowville, New York, an academy designed to give the greatest good to the greatest number under the observing eye of others in a Panopticon constructed building.

found in the struggle for good rules, this does not rise to the level of a guideline for living. It may be argued that seeking rules is the ethic, but the details of the rules accepted are arbitrary.

Any group of two or more living in proximity makes up rules for itself. This is the cultural basis for ethics. The problem arises when any member tries to make his or her rule transcendent without the agreement of others. The mere understanding that the group will not become combative over rules is a rule, perhaps the best rule there is. As in marriage, any group has to compromise, always extending tolerance to the rules of others. When this cannot be done, the group must disband and find members who will agree to whatever rules created the frisson in the first group.

Of course, ethical principles can comfortably be part of any religious doctrine. All religions have guiding principles, and adherence to these principles can be salutary and reassuring. If a Jewish Old Testament biblical commandment states, "Thou shalt not kill," this becomes a confessed belief. This admonition was created in a historical context. The people who did this were told the message was delivered by a deity speaking to their leader. This does not change its uncertainty as a guideline. As enduring as this rule is, there are religions that do not hold the same rule in the same esteem.

Any judgment over what is right and what is wrong (morality) can be configured in many ways. The conservative feels like conserving, while the liberal wants to allow for many possibilities. Once you safari through these terms, the realization is unavoidable that many conservatives have liberal aspects in their beliefs and many liberals have a number of conservative notions. In a political climate, it can be most difficult to define a person's values so that they fit neatly beneath one term or the other. Extremism can be viewed as a pathology in which a person requires others to conform to his or her beliefs.

When viewing very extremist views up close, such as those of the Nazis, Isis, or the Taliban, it is clear there is another motivation for these perspectives, a motivation other than the categories that the followers of these extreme ideas espouse. These groups have a general disdain and hate for others who won't join them. There is a gang mentality; life seems safer and more reasonable if you join the gang. If you have to destroy others to make the gang powerful, so be it. Many extremists are insecure people who require power to complete their senses of self. Close inspection of people such as Hitler, Pol Pot, Mao Tse-tung, Stalin, Kim Jong-il, and Charles Taylor reveal highly disturbed personalities who feel comfortable only after they have killed their presumed enemies, enemies in thought or in type. For these kinds of people, power is a seduction that allows behavior that would never be expressed in stabilized societies, but destabilized cultures allow these kinds of murderers to emerge. These people always exist, but when cultures begin to disintegrate, these despotic minds find a social path and expression, and their pathology is allowed to be fully expressed.

In a normal and healthy society, extremists must be suppressed for the safety of all. Placating them or conceding to them has no good outcome because their narcissistic power needs are the real subject of their discourse. Their perspective places no value in the general public good. Time and again in history, attempts by well-meaning diplomats and legislatures to bargain with these tyrants have proved fruitless. Sadly, society is sometimes forced to go to war.

EVIL

A brief comment regarding evil should be included. Evil is a Christian word emerging from a Christian mind-set. The myth of evil alludes to God's battle with the devil (the *d* shows his close connection to the concept of evil, as in *d-evil*). Its synonym is the phrase "really, really bad."

The question often arises as to whether a person is evil (with a capital *E*) or not. Is he or she so intrinsically bad that no forgiveness for this person is possible? Jeffrey Dahmer, the homosexual man who drugged potential lovers, cut off their heads, and kept them in the refrigerator, was called evil. In fact, he was a psychotic person with a fantasy regarding imbibing his victim's energy through cannibalism. Fictional Evil characters abound, like the cannibal Hannibal Lector (as in the first *Silence of the Lambs* movie, 1991), to the delight of horror-movie lovers. There is no need to recite these characters' crimes, as they are the crimes of the writer trying to titillate. Of course, all the aforementioned tyrants are evil. Their crimes are so vast and so heinous to the welfare of humanity that the word seems rightly applied.

Inherent in the concept of evil is the idea that it is an aberrancy of nature, it's intrinsic to the individual, and society needs the concept to label evil's perpetrators properly. The word can have any meaning society wants to apply to it, but the word has little edifying benefit. Calling someone evil has a ring to it. It's like a curse word, one of those words all languages have to express a severe feeling. Is there evil in the world? Well, the members of your culture say that, yes, there is evil. What do they mean? They mean that very terrible things are done by people to others. These extreme acts are beyond most of the world's acceptance, but evil is clearly a social construct. The fact that most of us can agree that certain acts may deserve the title of evil does not mean the word has any profound meaning. I've always been bemused that the Catholic Church never saw as Evil the French turning over Joan of Arc to the English for immolation as a female devil. This piece of history points out how culture-bound the term is. Evil exists, but it has meaning only in the eye of the beholder—just like beauty.

STATISTICS AS A MORALITY

As the scientific method has evolved, one value has emerged that needs some attention: truth as derived from a statistic. Another way of putting this is that a statistic is a kind of truth.

Without suggesting that I am an expert in the latest word in statistics, I can offer the finding that all statistics are a computation that shifts data toward some average. One adds the elements and divides that number into the number of characteristics being measured. A mathematical judgment is then made as to how far a particular element is from its usual characteristics. This is the foundation of all statistics. Whether using Chi Square, p values, k values, or just the mean (m), most of it is similar in meaning. What is ultimately obtained is always an approximate. The crucial question is how close that approximation is to a reality. In current statistical thinking, the estimate becomes almost as good as the absolute. When observers are not looking too closely, the estimate is declared an absolute, and all discussion centers around that finding as if it is truth itself.

Millions of dollars are earned and spent in scientific research using this perspective. Heads of departments, governments, research leaders, and business CEOs are appointed using these numbers. The stock market is governed in large part by this. I don't believe I can make a convincing argument decrying the use of statistics. Statistics are a large part of how the world functions now. However, I would like to emphasize the overconfidence that these approximations toward the means can create.

Many lectures in medicine, and psychiatry in particular, are designed to extol the virtues of this or that finding based on the numbers derived from a particular study. These studies are done on patients trying new drugs or on the incidence of side effects in drugs or in other measurable matters of importance. When findings from statistical studies show that a new drug has an edge over the efficacy of a placebo given at the same time to another set of patients, the finding becomes the argument for its being introduced into patient care. Psychiatrists know that these statistics are an uncertain finding. Their patients may not respond at all to the new drug, or the side effects may be overwhelming (and, in some cases, dangerous). The so-called phase 3 trials usually include around three thousand people. Despite this large number, the millions that ultimately get the new drug can react very differently than the trial participants did. Except with drugs that evince obvious effects, the giving of a new agent to millions of different people is daunting and uncertain. Psychiatry, using medicine, is based on estimations toward the means.

If ethics includes all value systems that dictate behavior, we would have to include statistics because the numbers derived from these exercises guide behavior. One of my favorite examples of this fallacy, and a simple one at that, is the teacher's assertion that if she did something special for one student, she would have to do it for all. "If I let one of you go home early because [insert a reason here], I would have to let you all go home early." The statistical principle here hides a premise that it's unfair to a class to give special treatment to a member of that class. Why is this premise considered true, and why is it applied indiscriminately to all cases, regardless of extenuating circumstances? You can easily imagine the harm this has done over the ages by teachers insensitive to special circumstances who insist on the undisclosed statistical rule. The alternative position is easy to state: "I will give you an exception in this circumstance because my parental position allows me to see that you require this. The class will simply have to accept the fact that exceptions are common in life."

This discussion of statistics has left out one of the most common errors in conclusions from scientific studies: the misidentification of a group when searching for a reasonable comparison. For example, schizophrenia is most difficult to define as an illness, and studies use agreed-upon definitions that may still be wrong. When people use the numbers that come from these studies, they presume everything has been done to homogenize the groups compared so that the statistics coming out of these findings may be valid. There is, for example, a special scored interview that purports to categorize people into different groups, one of them being that of schizophrenics. These interviews can be faulty because they can depend entirely on the experience of the interviewers. They can be based on questions that are faulty; or they can be based on conclusions leading to the diagnoses that can be faulty. The degree of uncertainty is great. However, eager academicians needing advancement may minimize these problems. As long as the standardized tests are being used, the findings are accepted by the majority of academia. This amounts to fault piled on fault. The statistical findings become a kind of emotional romance among participants in which all agree to abide by the rules while the rules may not apply properly. These agreements lead to a fantasy that investigations are always dealt with on a factual plane and that findings are valuable. This is often a chimera designed for nothing more than personal advancement.

Currently, there is a paradigm that statistics are a valid way of finding truth. When this paradigm shifts, as it must, many will be out of a job. For decades there was a belief in ether as the medium through which light travels. Through difficult experiments, Michelson and Morely showed there was no ether. Imaginative Einstein took this fact, among others, and changed the way we saw the universe.

The field of statistics has limited value, although it is not without value. The estimates and sampling in the procedures of statistics demand humility, but humility is not what is currently seen in the academic world. In a sampling of a thousand subjects resulting in a statistical value with a $p=.05$, there is a less than 5 percent chance that the results would come from chance. How many studies have later been done on ten thousand that show that the results of the thousand were faulty because of sample size? This doesn't even include the mistake of a wrong definition when identifying what should be sampled. The meaning of all this is? Statistics is often no better a way of making value judgments than group consensus.

This is not to say there is no value in statistics. Like the humble ruler, statistics is a measurement tool that helps in determining things. The key word is *helps*. No statistic is a final solution; it's merely a pointer toward a solution. If 60 percent do it and 40 percent do not do it, then more people do it; the conclusion that it's better to be among the 60 or worse to be among the 40 is untenable. Advertisers heavily lean on this fallacious idea. If a TV show gathers a certain percentage of the audience, the show is retained for the following year. The cutoff is determined by the commercial values of those invested in the show. *Star Trek* had a terrible statistic for many years but was kept on the air through the doggedness of its creator. Its followers multiplied, and the *Star Trek* franchise is history.

How to use a statistic is a judgment call. The numbers may point, but they do not describe. The details are where the values lie, not in the numbers. The error of taking numbers and jumping to conclusions is widespread.

CONCLUSIONS ABOUT MORALITY

If morality is culturally biased, how is right and wrong to be determined? Simply speaking, this is an unsolvable conundrum. Accepting there is no universal given of right or wrong, putting aside the religious conviction, and appreciating the language confusion inherent in these value terms, we are left with the culture in which we developed. This is not necessarily a bad thing. For the most part, agreeing to abide by the cultural norms is adaptive. If my culture says killing is bad and I accept this, I will probably live comfortably within my given world. If I deny this cultural belief, I will most likely get into a great deal of trouble. Finding inconsistencies in values is the norm. Not killing cannot always be right, but it is mostly right in this culture. Adapting to the norms but keeping an open mind about their ambiguities and inconsistences is the most comfortable and healthiest way to live. It may come as a surprise to many that living within given cultural rules while not completely believing in any of them works very well. This is recommended.

There are no absolutes in morality because all morality is made of presumptions by humans. For centuries right and wrong had biblical and koranic sanctification. There were people and moralities quite different before the Jews and before the Muslims. Many tribal groups have vastly different values than Western. The rules we are to follow are the rules we were born into. That's it. All the rest is commentary on culture.

AESTHETICS

Like truth, reality, the good, and the bad, much has been made of the idea of the beautiful. Most would agree that a sunset is beautiful when over a mountain lake with clouds to catch the oranges and purples. A cynic might point out that the same sunset, on the same earth, as seen through the pipes and towers of a petroleum plant, is not beautiful.

What is beautiful? In a word, it's a word. I'm sure you're not surprised by this conclusion by now. Moreover, it's a value-laden word and therefore finds itself in the company of ethics. Even so, the idea of the beautiful requires some discussion. All of human art depends on an inspection of the term and its parent concept, the aesthetic.

Assessment is intrinsic to life. We are always evaluating what is worth keeping and what should be discarded. Making aesthetic judgments is done to help communicate the value of the created product. Clearly, these judgments are human bound. There is no absolute aesthetic, but there is purpose, meaning, and value in determining the captivating quality of any production.

Of course, the "captivating quality of any production" refers to art. Art is a most difficult matter to explain, let alone define. One perspective is that art is any humanly created item designed to communicate the spirit of the person making it. You can see at once that this explanation allows a broad range of latitude regarding what is art. This is how it should be.

Any visit to a modern museum of art challenges the viewer. Strings hanging from ceilings, videos super-imposed one on another, computer patterns with variegated colors, plastic models of toys blown up to massive proportions to startle, and canvases of light pencil lines drawn parallel to one another on white paint are all "art." The traditional paintings of Rembrandt, Vermeer, and David are also art. The sculpture of Brancusi with his original shapes and Rodin's illustrating the angst of humanity boldly outlined in bronze also is declared art. Is it possible to declare one is better than the other? One deserves to be conserved and the other discarded? Can one say confidently that Koons is not worthy, but Veronese is?

No. It is impossible to place values here. Art is an expression, a communication, and it can take many forms. The community of viewers decides. The museum curator decides. Posterity decides. The individual looking at a challenging communication in the form of a declared art cannot defend the position that the art is not worthy of its declaration. If it's on display as art—if someone decided it should be seen in a museum or in a loft or in someone's home—then it has to be considered art. There is no way to argue otherwise.

In the community of art, critics have the job of assessing value. This is often useful. It is impossible for everyone to see the art extant and evaluate what seems valuable and what does not. Critics serve a most needed purpose, bringing their expertise and specialization to the rest of us. They give some sense of what might be worth experiencing. This does not mean the critic can make an accurate statement of what item is worth more than another. The critic can only make a statement; it's up to the rest of us to follow that or not. Often we find critics' comments very useful, and they bring us to art that is worth our time; other times we disagree. There is no right here.

As a lover of music, I can tell you that I have a severe bias that Bach, Mozart, Beethoven, Brahms, and Shostakovich are greater than Lady Gaga, Madonna, or Justin Bieber. However, I cannot defend this bias. The bias is built up over years of training in classical music and a comparatively passing interest in these popular singers. I know, however, there are aficionados of popular music who find deep and abiding meaning in the poetry and tonalities of the genre. I cannot argue with them. The fact that it takes training to appreciate fully the art of Rembrandt and Bach only declares the seeming truth that it's difficult for the idle listener to easily appreciate the greatness of these composers. It cannot mean that they are superior. Bias does not bring forth truth.

A sunset over a mountain lake is nearly a universally agreed upon scene of beauty. There do seem to be elements of art that deserve the term *beauty* to be applied. Again, this becomes a social convention. We are humans designed by nature to like sexual congress, and we are designed by nature to agree on a sense of beauty in certain experiences. Beauty becomes a bias, not an absolute. Anyone who pursues beauty as an absolute and insists on using it as criteria for what is valuable in art is doomed to failure.

There seems to be an indefensible posture when comparing art. The inclination to make a symphony superior to a popular song cannot be satisfied. This does not mean that the meaning of art, the attempt to show why a certain production is special, should be discarded. Graffiti cannot be judged inferior to Jasper Johns; there are, however, curatorial reasons why a Johns may be preferred in a museum over an art production from a subway wall. These reasons may or may not be convincing, but they follow critical discipline and study. Similarly, a demonstration of how a Bach prelude has a profound resonance with the human soul deserves attention. Over many years, certain art forms stand out and are repeatedly absorbed by generations. The quality that makes this happen should absorb our attention. You may not win a battle arguing the Beatles beats Bach, but the output of Bach and his work's celestial grandeur deserve to be studied and enjoyed.

Perhaps the market speaks better than any argument. Many say, "I may not be able to explain it, but I know what I like." This describes the art market, especially when you add the idea of what is valuable for purchase. The cost placed on pictorial art depends much on the stories behind each piece. The fact that Rothko left picture drawing to find the power of color combinations and committed suicide in the process makes his art of value to many. The configurations of Pollack, who died in an alcohol-related car accident, sell well. The misery of Pollack and Rothko, however, are an embellishment to those who find their depictions challenging and invigorating. Still, their works would be hard to defend as significantly better than Monet's.

The sensible person can only enter into the art world with humility and a willingness to learn. He or she stands back while others demand that this picture or this literature is superior to others. At the same time, wisdom requires that we try very hard to appreciate what tradition and intelligent criticism have found important. The world of art warrants a wide-ranging appreciation of the different manifestations of communication. The communication may be on the canvas or in the story behind the canvas, but it is always communication. As Californians are wont to say, "It speaks to me." This does not mean it is superior art. The poetry may speak to you and be doggerel. Training and an open mind are required to tell the difference. Shakespeare is not an easy read and does not always speak to someone, but it nearly always rewards study.

In the final word, beauty and art are difficult to define. Training helps distinguish between the momentary pleasure of a thing and the deep, life-giving meaning of a work. The open mind does not remain at the level of ignorance and the obvious. All of us should be able to enjoy the music of Random Access Memory as well as a Shostakovich quartet. We may not be able to defend beauty and great art, but we will have a keen sense of what we are talking about. We feel the preference. Our time of life, our social settings, our educations will all play a part in our choices. Furthermore, as with any language, with study and knowledge, we begin to understand what the artist is trying to say. Knowing the artist's meaning may be easy, as in popular art, or difficult, as in curatorial art. Both seem a worthwhile part of our culture. Woe unto anyone who wishes to demonstrate that *easy art* is inferior to *hard art*.

Something must be said about the great importance of including aesthetic endeavors in one's life. These endeavors can be as a participating artist (amateur or professional), or as someone enjoying art as an observer. Though the arts in the form of music, drawing and painting, drama, literature, or sculpture may not be everyone's cup of tea, the importance of appreciating aesthetics in some form cannot be overstated. We may not be able to defend the position that hard art is better intrinsically than easy art, but we should place emphasis on the enormous satisfactions to be derived from studying and improving one's appreciation of art. Understanding the importance of perspective makes a painting more enjoyable. For example, the naïve cannot look at the Vermeer of *The Artist's Studio* and enjoy the play of one view over another unless trained to look intelligently at the painting. Pollock's color schemes are intelligent and coherent, but it is necessary to study color arrangements and combinations to fully enjoy what seems at first to be smears and scribbles of paint. It is necessary to get used to Shakespearian poetry and prose to enjoy his observations and textual brilliance. The sense of peculiarity in sixteenth- and seventeenth-century drama has to be conquered before the magnificence of Shakespeare can be enjoyed. Playing and studying Bach makes the music come alive. Before the *Rite of Spring* can be fully appreciated beyond its percussive expressiveness, it is necessary to learn about Stravinsky's design, the work's roots in Russian music and myths, and its deviation from the standard music of the first part of the twentieth century.

Life is enhanced by art. Ignoring its contribution is to take all the color out of the day-to-day world. Immersing oneself in an art form, be it craft or new creations, is one of the great satisfactions in our existence. There is no reason to be elitist about this. Actively participating in any art form—even operating with a low level of expertise in the smallest part of the endeavor—changes a person. This person feels life has a meaning that it did not have without art. The aesthetic may not fully be a *raison d'etre*, but it is always an enhancement. A life without art is a life without spirit. The sensible life always includes aesthetics.

PSYCHIATRY

Psychiatry is a word made of *psyche* and *-iatry*. Psyche was the spirit of life for the ancient Greeks, their kind of soul. The suffix *-iatry* means *to treat or render care*. Psychiatry is the treatment of the soul. Since soul and mind are often conflated, the word attaches to treatment of the mind. Psychologists also treat the mind, but they usually don't deal with its medical biology with the same intensity.

The practice of psychiatry can be divided into two treatment categories. The first is human-to-human treatments during which the psychiatrist uses persuasion and the doctor-patient relationship to help the patient. This is psychotherapy. The second is medical treatment of various forms, using drugs, magnetism, electroconvulsive therapy, and, in very rare instances, surgery. There is no surprise in the fact that each side of this division attracts different kinds of people as well as a few that live comfortably on both sides.

Psychiatry is an imperfect discipline with diverse advocates for its various treatments. Since most treatments are a mixture of effectiveness and ineffectiveness, there is a large domain in which the unscrupulous can operate. Most psychiatrists are very caring and work with a high level of interest in the welfare of the patient, but they all have personalities and histories that render them more or less effective. Some are enthusiastic for drug treatment; others are just as ardent for psychotherapy. The average, well-meaning practitioner uses whatever he or she can to render some improvement in the troubled or ill.

In the struggle to establish the field as legitimate, researchers have exaggerated the solidity of the diagnoses and the certainty of certain treatments. Over the past thirty years, schizophrenia has remained a puzzle. Bipolar mood disorder is barely beginning to expose its secrets, and there is a great deal of muddling over hyperactivity disorders, anxiety, and even depression. Most psychiatrists can distinguish these categories better than the uninitiated, but they also find themselves in a daily uncertainty about them. The Diagnostic and Statistical Manual for Mental Disorders 5 (DSM-5) barely helps. Despite its official nature and the endorsement of the American Psychiatric Association, the standards and guidelines are not universally agreed upon. At best, the manual delineates the disorders of interest and provides a cultural consensus on how to look upon mental and emotional disorders. There is nothing definitive about it.

Unlike the disorders such as pneumonia or diabetes, the symptoms of which lead clearly to identification of cause and treatment, schizophrenia, depression, and anxiety can be misdiagnosed.

Schizophrenia is often mistaken for bipolar disorder or depression. Someone diagnosed with anxiety may actually have depression and may respond to antidepressant drugs. Depression can be a physical illness. These diagnoses in DSM are chameleon-like, changing form in different contexts. Depression can present mainly with anxiety. The categories do not equal fundamentally different entities. Mistakes in research are easy to make, and the application of drugs can confound the practitioner.

Medicine made a major advance with the nineteenth century. The cell was discovered to be the source of disease, and a lesion in it was the framework upon which medicine developed. Clearly, the cell as the primary source of difficulty does not hold up as well in psychiatry. The cell is left far behind, for the most part, when considering the mind. Medicine advanced further when evidence indicated physiological or functional disorders of specific types. The discovery of infection and chemical metabolic errors, which allow a broader and more extensive understanding of human physical misery, advanced medicine still further. However, in a discipline in which behavior and feeling is prominent, the mind remained largely uncharted.

Psychiatry is largely stuck with descriptions, and descriptions are prone to all the maladies of ambiguous language. One may argue about virus or bacterial causes for illness, but the evidence remains that there is some category of infection. In psychiatry, the underlying process is largely a mystery, and there is no element in all the diagnoses that can account for the illness. The doctor is left with a vague picture of what is happening and applies vague drugs and uncertain medical behaviors toward treating the event. Simply because a drug is labeled "antidepressant" does not mean the drug is acting directly on a depression in part of the brain. It is highly unlikely there is such a place. Though there is some evidence serotonin or norepinephrine is low in depressives, there is contrary data that suggests this is not the main feature of the illness. Doctors ardently try to match the drug to the patient, but the matching remains tentative at best. The desperate search for biological markers for psychiatric illnesses remains unsatisfied.

The reaction to this is sometimes mistakenly extreme. Many possess an exaggerated complete skepticism toward the field. In *The Myth of Mental Illness,* Thomas Szasz[5] claims doctors contrive illnesses that don't exist. This position did a lot of harm. Patient sufferings were put aside and seen as a social dysfunction. One view argued that the illness was actually a projection of the psychiatrist's need to control the patient. Other pundits posited that there was no suffering in the first place. Culture won that brief tempest, but there is general agreement now that people do suffer, and the misery should be studied so that solutions can be found to ameliorate these conditions. All practicing physicians now agree there are mental illnesses; the effects of these disorders are measurable and costly. Exactly what they are and the best way to help patients is the debatable issue. All responsible psychiatrists know this and live with the humility of not being able to solve many of the problems that come before them. Politicizing mental illness serves little purpose and is often very harmful.

At the center of these controversies is the so-called mind-body problem. Is it the diseased mind that is at the seat of personal misery? Is there a specific physical abnormality that must be discovered? Alternatively, is it illness as understood by Freud, with its familial pathologies and its maldeveloped childhood that is at the root of most psychological suffering? Is the body-brain in which the mind rests disordered or chemically in disarray? Is it this biological disarray that creates depression, or is it family conflicts?

The reasonable professional sees a combination. Sometimes the illness follows a pattern that clearly designates a body disorder. A sudden irruption into extravagant madness is a body dysfunction. This manic

---

5   Thomas Szasz, *The Myth of Mental Illness* (New York: Harper and Roe, 1974).

behavior likely comes from a genetic abnormality that makes moods labile and extravagant, the so-called bipolar disorder. Ironically, however, the eruption itself might be stimulated by conflicts and stresses in daily life. In this case, the mind in conflict affects the body, urging its propensity for chemical malfunctioning to express itself. In other cases, excitability and aggressiveness can come from child abuse. With a few drinks or certain drugs (e.g., cocaine), a person at a public bar can seem so overly verbal and aggressive that his or her agitation over a minor slight can look like mania. The abnormal behavior, however, is a result of developed anger with a little outside chemical nudge. Here, understanding requires an appreciation of that developmental history. Stress and current psychological states play a large role.

Diagnoses are ambiguous at best. Treatment is no better. There is no clear evidence that one treatment is superior to another. There are studies that support drugs as a treatment for psychosis and depression, but they are not more than 60 to 70 percent confident. There are also studies that indicate psychotherapy is effective. The certainty of this is even lower than treatment with drugs. All psychotherapies (psychodynamic, cognitive, behavioral, dialectic, and others) depend largely on the quality of the interpersonal relationship between the patient and the therapist. This has been well established. If the patient trusts the doctor to be well meaning and caring, he or she responds positively. This can be viewed either as a placebo effect, independent of the nature of the therapy being used, or a statement of the power of human support.

Despite these uncertainties in treatment, a number of technical features stand out. The importance of the unconscious, the importance of transference, and the significance of historical issues continue to be fundamental issues in the patient's current life. These are all significant and essential considerations in caring for patients.

Behaviorists, dependent on the theory of habituation and rein-forcement (both valuable concepts), ignore these psychodynamic elements. The psychodynamic clinician must also be aware of be-havioral and surface interpersonal matters, but these are usually not neglected to the same degree as the unconscious, transference, and historical development. The recent hostility to Freudian ideas has led to the belief that these matters can be ignored. This position is that concepts such as habits, automatic thinking, and environmental re-inforcements can be used to treat in isolation without attention to developmental and familial concerns. Here behaviorists use a part of the human situation, conditioning, to explain everything, focusing only on the here and now. Though the conditioning is historical, it is compartmentalized to include only the environmental factors leading to the faulty habits via training. The unconscious familial problems are underappreciated.

No therapist can ignore developmental pathologies and still fully help the patient. Though behaviorists pay lip service to the importance of the unconscious, transference, and family history, the difficulties with parents, siblings, and even self-image are rated lower in importance for the formation of the maladaptive habits accumulated. The cognitive therapist is also interested in current ideas in the patient's mind that lead to poor life outcomes. More often than not, the cognitive therapist minimizes early childhood difficulties.

The mind is largely unconscious. For the most part, our three-pound brains function independently of our awareness. While we learn a new task, we are aware of the learning struggle but have little knowledge of the protein changes, the synaptic receptor changes, and neuronal pathway changes. These are all unconscious. Our hearts, lungs, kidneys, blood flow, cellular battles, and general metabolism are all going on in the brain outside of awareness.

The brain is processing millions of bits of information before our conscious minds are alert to the significance of the same information. Emotional experiences have their impact immediately, but the impact may continue hours, days, and even months after they occur. The very idea of posttraumatic stress disorder demands a conviction. This belief is that there is an unconscious dealing with the severe discomfort of an event. We think we are stable and at ease in our aware selves while the mind in the brain grapples with the events of the trauma. The notion that only 20 percent of a person's mind is conscious seems about right. Our brains are working outside of our awareness 80 percent of the time.

Transference is a Freudian concept. It is also an important principle of human interaction that can be applied to daily life. When humans relate, they are not only dealing with the here and now, but also with the historical past that makes up who they are. If the interaction is lasting and meaningful, humans have a tendency to place on other people feelings or ideas that were originally applied to parents or siblings. When someone behaves in a certain way to another person, this behavior may be similar to what that person experienced earlier with a parent or sibling. The feeling is that the new event is fresh but uncomfortable, and this discomfort relates to the past experience more than it relates to the behavior experienced in front of him or her. When this merging of past and present occurs, the behavior is called transference. The individual transfers the feelings from the past onto the person in the present. There is no awareness of this. In therapy this occurs when a patient complains of qualities in the therapist that hark back to these same qualities in a parent or sibling. This is a transference of beliefs regarding an earlier person onto the one in the relationship.

We are all historical animals. We are not only managing the moment, but also the past. Relationships from the past help form our beliefs and attitudes; these are then projected onto significant current relationships. The unconscious does this automatically, and when neither party is aware of the transference process, the conflicts in the relationship can cause a rift. In therapy, a good therapist is always aware of this and uses it to help the patient. The positive side of transference is the patient's admiring of the therapist and working well with him or her to the patient's benefit. In this case, trust comes easily. The negative side of transference is the patient's mistrust if he or she suffered childhood abuse. In relationships, in general, transference is always operating to some extent. An awareness of this encourages the security of the relationship while undermining its negative influences.

Finally, the therapist must never deny the importance of the historical influences on the patient. Mother and Father are powerful and god-like. The brain is malleable in those first five years, and parents teach the child language, manners, control, culture, and a worldview. A Japanese child in Japan learns Japanese. A Japanese child in the United States learns American English. The child learns religion from the parents. The child also learns conflict and maladaptation from the parents. The maladaptation can take the form of the same abusive behavior experienced in the family. The victim has difficulty negotiating all relations in life. The abused child, then, is suffering from the abuse forever.

None of these issues can be ignored in understanding another person. Culture, language, beliefs, habits, self-image, and all human interaction are part of the early childhood experiences. Nonhistorical therapy is doomed to failure. More importantly, an individual who doesn't come to terms with the unsettled issues of childhood will never have a comfortable and meaningful life.

These three concepts, the unconscious, transference, and the psychological history of the individual, have to be the bedrock of any therapy. Good behaviorists know this and incorporate them into their work, just as a psychodynamic therapist incorporates behavioral concepts.

It is unfortunate that the complexity of helping people leads to specialization. Human beings are both animals and people. The work of the horse whisperer may well work on the animal part of a human being while not proving effective to the person side. Analyzing stress and its indelible effects on human habits is important. Changing the automatic ideas that affect behavior (the domain of the cognitive therapist) should be applied. All the therapeutic techniques available are preferred in different situations at different times. There are many reasons why these approaches are splintered and put into separate categories. These reasons have to do with professional preferences, time required for training, individual comfort, and cost. However, arguing for the exclusivity of one over the other is a worthless enterprise; when trying to help patients, exclusivity of practice style is counterproductive.

THE MIND-BODY CONFLICT

The brain is extremely complicated. Let us take a side road for a brief discussion in order to impress ourselves just how complicated it is.

There are billions of neurons packed into three pounds of gelatinous mass. Each of these living neurons is a cell and has trillions of interconnections called synapses. Imagine two long cells nearly touching, but stopping short of a gap between them. This is the synapse. This space is very tiny, but it is the highway of communication between nerve cells. The presynaptic neuron, the giver, the one sending the message, is not a simple conduit for an electric charge. It contains bubbles, or vesicles of complex chemicals, called transmitters. These vesicles, upon getting an electric signal from the nerve, travel to the edge near the synapse and then "pop" into the space, sending the chemicals to the postsynaptic or receiver nerve. This receiver nerve is highly complex as well. It contains chemical receptors made up of "gates" of proteins in its membranes. These receptors allow the sending neuron's chemicals to affect the entire nerve cell receiving the transmission.

There are many different kinds of receptors, such as serotonin receptors, dopamine receptors, and others. They operate to allow chemical connections within the interior of the cell, and this interior transmits the electric signals down its length to the next receiver cells and the next synapse. Each receptor is enormously complex, consisting of intricately twisted proteins that bind, according to very specific chemical and geometrical rules, to another molecule in the synapse. This allows charged particles in a surrounding fluid to enter the cell. From these atomic particles (called ions), the cell's metabolism changes, and this activity activates the cell for transmission. One nerve cell can have many synapses along its length. The transmission of the electric signal is not anything like that of a copper wire in a circuit. It consists of a complex electrical current that is briefly sustained by the influx and outflow of potassium, calcium, and sodium (ions) along its length.

The brain is quite structured. The nerves of the thinking part, the so-called cortex, are layered with different kinds of cells. Research has shown that there is a primary memory area called the hippocampus (because some think it's shaped like a horse) in a specific area of the dentate gyrus. However, this is not the only place where memory is placed using special proteins; memory is distributed throughout the brain. The brain has been conveniently compartmentalized for the sake of investigation, but it is clear that all areas are connected in some way.

In addition to these transmitter neurons, there are many other cells that have the job of cleaning and nurturing the environment around the transmitters. Their job seems important and is just beginning to be understood. How much they play into the resulting *mind* is yet to be determined. One cell, for example, makes an extended sheath that covers the transmitter neurons and makes them send their message faster. This sheath, called myelin, is complex and plays its role in neuronal efficiency.

This is a mere snapshot of the complexity of this organ called the brain, but this snapshot is important because it belies the idea that brain activities are merely electrical. On the contrary, the complexity of the brain's activity is enormous. From this organ comes the *mind*. You cannot have a mind without this organ.

This doesn't mean that the mind, the thinking part of our consciousness that tells us who we are, where we are, and organizes our memory of everything, is merely brain matter. We cannot extrapolate at this time from the neurons, brain organization, and internal chemistry to *mind*. Arguing that *mind* is merely an organic manifestation of brain activity is as foolish as arguing that *mind* is something that transcends neuronal, synaptic, and chemical activity. We don't know what the mind is, even if we feel some confidence talking about it as if it were specifically something. The clear fact that you cannot have a mind without the brain does not settle this issue. The brain can be the foundation of the mind just as hydrogen and oxygen are the foundations of water. Each element does not itself explain water, while we are very confident that you need each to have water. Like water, the brain has constituents, but their operation in combination defies the concept of *mind*. We are best keeping the uncertainty at this level for now, though as we explore the brain, we are sure to come closer and closer to appreciating the connection between brain and mind.

The mind-brain problem remains a problem of language. Mind seems disembodied from the brain. We do not think in terms of neuronal transmissions—we think *thoughts*. We are married to our words, and words come from language. Words tell us we have a mind, but the words are vague, ineffable, and uncertain. Language becomes a dark closet that provides an illusion of confidence.

Mind, soul, psyche, and spirit are terms that are impossible to explicate fully, yet we somehow feel sure they mean something. The problem is not choosing one word over another, mind verses brain for example. All terms remain ambiguous; the problem is understanding that we apply words to the idea of mind and then think that is the end of the discussion. It is not. Using mind we downplay the organic source as the brain. Using brain we don't see the full expression of the mind and its psychological and social ramifications. The worst thing we can do is underplay the importance of the language dilemma when arguing for or against either side of the question. Linguistically speaking, we are both mind and brain.

Surely, more research will reveal more understanding of the workings of the brain. Perhaps discoveries will reveal how the brain transforms into the feeling we have about mind. (Analogously, we may someday understand the atomic transformations that allow electrons shared by hydrogen and two oxygens to be changed into water, that essential fluid for life.) Only then will we be able to fully resolve the mind-brain issue. Perhaps we will say, "This degree of neuronal activity in this place is the necessary ingredient for us to feel integrated with a mind." Until then, it is essential to respect the linguistic dichotomy. Mind and brain are essential separate concepts for working with people. We know they are connected, but the full connectivity is yet to be understood.

The importance of appreciating that the mind-body confusion is a language issue cannot be overstated. (In psychiatric parlance, the phrase "mind-body" is often used interchangeably with "mind-brain" as I've done here. The brain is seen as "body" in these discussions.) A feeling that the word *mind* or *consciousness* has meaning is insufficient to clarify which is which. It's hard to ignore the idea that mind comes from brain, but that does not solve the problem. It is our thinking processes that create the dichotomy. Only continued scientific investigation will help clarify how one construct (mind) plays upon the other (brain) and vice versa. While we wait, it is most important that we see the value of either side of the equation. We can appreciate psychological processes without alluding to neuronal activity and appreciate the brain without dealing with consciousness or mind. Both the brain and mind can be understood when they interact in ways that show mutual dependence. This is merely another temporary resolution, similar to the religious conflation of the Son, the Father, and the Holy Ghost. However, in this case, we can find the solution without dying.

DREAMS

Freud thought that his most monumental contribution to psychology was his interpretation of dreams. From this brilliant investigation, he developed the concept of the typographical structure of the mind. For Freud, dreams came from the unconscious and emerged as stories representing conflicts allowed expression in the twilight of wakefulness. The fully alert mind acted as a censor to erase the painful anxieties associated with the images the unconscious mind developed. While lying on the couch, this censor had to be set aside through free association, and the analyst would help check the censor through interpretation. When the conflicts were made known to the suffering person, this awareness would help in his or her cure.

This dynamic push-pull idea of dreams still holds some influence in psychological circles. However, an understanding of dreams remains unfulfilled, and there is much debate about Freud's use of this aspect of the mind.

The brain can be viewed as a story-telling organ. When we sleep, it makes up tales, and these are often complex and amazing in their elaborate reference to aspects of our lives. Whether the stories represent conflicts or are merely conflating images and experiences from our daily lives remains uncertain. The fact remains that in sleep our brains contrive the most fascinating narrative imaginable. Image flits to image, thought to thought, and we in our somnolence have little or no control over the matter. It is from this dynamic that Freud felt the dream was the royal road to the unconscious.

Dreams may or not be the royal road to the unconscious, but the images and stories contained in them still assist the physician with understanding likely themes of importance to the patient. No one can use a dream to foretell the future as did Joseph for the pharaoh, but from dreams we can discover clues that lead to important issues in a person's life.

In large part, dreams are related physically to REM (rapid eye movement) sleep. The eyes move back and forth as if the person is watching a movie or television, but the story the person sees is one created by the sleeping brain. Fragments of images probably come from sleep without REM (NREM), but these do not have the narrative form. This is as far as investigations have come in connecting brain with sleep activity. REM is detected by EEG (electroencephalographic) lines on a moving paper. These lines are created by electrical signals made by brain that are sent via wires placed on the skull. Heart rate, breathing rate, blood pressure, and muscle activity are all measured as well. Diminished body movement (a so-called paradoxical paralysis) and heightened physiological activity (heart rate, blood pressure, and breathing speed) have all been associated with dreams. The essential part of brain narrative remains unexplained.

The amazing story-telling brain has answers, but we do not yet know them. Dreams are fascinating and intriguing. They most certainly mean something in the living mind. Therapists use them with uncertainty, but they seem to be helpful when trying to understand someone's life issues. The meaning of many dreams still remain beyond confident reach, a source of extensive speculation with partial understanding. Some dreams are transparent and clearly relate to waking conflicts. Experience helps unravel these blankets of care, but not all can be made clear.

PSYCHOSOMATICS

Psychosomatic medicine is the discipline in which the psychological (mind) factors and the body interact to give rise to disease. Of course this very much includes the brain. The sensory system (hearing, seeing, and touch) is the connection between the environment and the body, and the information the world provides enters the brain through these mediums. The brain translates this information in various ways. One translation converts the signals into body messages.

For the most part, environment leaves the body relatively unaffected. The pulse may rise and fall when a person takes an exam. The blood pressure may elevate when there is a family argument and then quickly return to normal. The body and the brain usually maintain a balance, or homeostasis. When the information from the outside world is so toxic that homeostasis cannot be continued, the body reactions are extreme and can damage the organs. This equation of environmental stress and body disorder is the essence of psychosomatics.

It is clear from this that stress is a major concern when trying to understand how the world affects the mind and body. However, the significance of any particular stress is not always easy appreciate. One person's body may react to a minor argument in a severe way, while another person's body may not react much at all to the same argument. Something that looks toxic to one observer may not be toxic to another. For this reason, it is most difficult to list stresses for all.

Resilience is a companion concept that is hard to define. Each individual has different capacities of resistance to stress experiences, and these capacities depend on genetics and early life influences. People from strong families tend to handle stress better. Those with severe conflicts and childhood abuse, for example, tend to handle stress with more difficulty.

Many have attempted to quantify what stresses cause the most trouble, regardless of resilience. Some authors have come up with the idea of "life-change units" in an attempt to predict what life experiences might be more likely to cause disorders or disease. The number of units is proportional to the negative effect a life experience might have on someone. Death of a child or spouse has a large number and heads the list of likely causes of body changes. Other less potent stresses have been the sale of a house, getting married, or exams. As controversial as the idea of life-change units might be, it remains a strong application indicating that life difficulties can cause body changes and even disease. Studies support this view, and people with high life-change units have been found to visit doctors more and to have more physical problems. This idea remains controversial but interesting.

Depression has been shown to worsen outcomes of heart disease. Family dysfunction often plays a role in asthma attacks. Marital conflicts have been associated with a worsening course of colitis or arthritis. Severe insomnia often occurs from posttraumatic stress disorder. The list of stress-related illnesses (or worsening of illnesses) is very long. Suffice it to say that stress in everyday life is contributory toward the manifestation of illness and disease.

One can make a line across the page that represents all human diseases. At the left end are those disorders that arise out of psychological stresses, such as job tension, family discord, and threatening work. From these aggravations may come headaches, muscle pain, insomnia, and other reversible discomforts. The middle of the line may include asthma, arthritis, hypertension, and other illnesses where the body susceptibility and the stresses overlap in their causal importance. At the far right are those illnesses that have increasingly genetic and physical (e.g., infection) contributions. This illustration helps to demonstrate that all illness may be usefully placed along a spectrum in which environment and body interact to varying degrees. This becomes not so much a matter of either (outside world or body), but more a matter of how much each contributes to the outcome.

The field of psychosomatic medicine is of great interest. What is missing is a clear idea of how stress transforms into illness. We cannot predict that a given stressful situation guarantees a body disorder. Generally, we can say that so much stress *might* lead to illness, but not that it predictably will. This is the unknown in the field. Perhaps, in the future, a particular identifiable genome with be delineated to show that a certain person should not be a pilot or is particularly susceptible to certain life experiences. This certainly is not the case currently, and we are left with the overall idea that life experiences and body are extremely connected. Our task is to understand how.

This realization means that stress, in general, should be minimized. A life with shift work, high tension (e.g., nuclear missile silo duty), combat, or daily threats of job dismissal (to mention merely a few) is likely to give early-onset illness and perhaps a shortened life span. Stress can be severely damaging, but is not always so. Given the findings in psychosomatic medicine in the context of a patient's wish to live as long a life as possible, the premise that stress is to be avoided is probably a good one.

Any planning for a good and sensible life has to keep this in mind. Days of retirement should have just enough tension to keep the mind tuned and the body in good shape, but no more. When possible, family conflicts should be resolved. Lifelong hates should be dispelled. Parental and sibling grievances have to be put into a place of quiet, acceptance, or settlement. A person's adaptation to his or her financial state is crucial.

Psychosomatics emphasizes the underrated fact that we are sensitively intertwined with our environments. The outside sensory awareness of the living body is more delicate than appreciated. The sound of traffic, for example, can be damaging even though the person in question has no awareness of the stressor. In one study, children's reading scores were lower the closer the high-rise building's floors were to the traffic below. No one was ever aware before of how the unconscious sense of traffic could act as a stress.

A minor argument can have similar effects. The agitation from a heated discussion can raise blood pressure, increase the pulse, and put some stress on the heart, for example, though the body can quickly compensate. In an already injured heart, more serious consequences can occur. Though this reaction to stress is common knowledge it is often not appreciated. The body is a sensitive receiver of all environmental stimuli. Sensory input from wind, temperature, relationships, and sounds is constantly received and translated by the body into various responses. It would be a vast error to neglect this intermingling. Stress becomes the measure or construct through which this is understood. Its full significance is just beginning to be appreciated.

The body is never alone. The brain is never alone. The world of people and sensations of many kinds always affect the body. Its homeostasis is dependent on the DNA resilience of all of its organs. The brain, for the most part, translates these stimuli into body activity. This is done through the core brain, the limbic systems with its hypothalamic regulatory systems. Even watching a movie can alter internal body functioning. Psychosomatics is always with us.

The mixing of the world and the person's reactions is ever present. The image of the candle flame responding to the slightest breath is a useful example. Light blowing merely results in a flickering that quickly returns to normal. A heavy blowing puts the candle out. It behooves the person trying to live the sensible life to always keep in mind that the mind and the body are just like the candle flame. We are always part of the blowing world. Every effort must be made to keep the interaction within healthy bounds.

DRUGS

Drugs are a mainstay of psychiatry and even help to define the identity of the psychiatrist. Patients, in general, have an overwhelming belief in their efficacy. These two elements make using drugs in treating emotionally troubled people a problem.

Drugs are tools with limits and are given in a semiblind fashion to help. When a drug is developed, its side effects and dangers are investigated as much as is possible, but this investigation is always limited. Most drug trials do not examine more than three thousand to five thousand people. The complexity of humans is so great that this sample usually turns out to be insufficient. When drugs are released for use and approved by the United States Food and Drug Administration, they are largely unknown in their effects on the greater population. Every doctor knows that the new drug on the block can operate in unpredictable ways. After all, three thousand is not a reasonable fraction of seven billion.

While the drug is not fully known, the patient taking the drug is known even less. The human body has been researched extensively and remains a black box of internal operations. Extensive knowledge is available, but this knowledge is usually insufficient to predict comfortably what a drug is going to do. Though repeated use of an agent gives the doctor some confidence, he or she cannot predict how a patient will respond.

Currently, there is a lot of interest in genome differences to drug response. Some tests are now available to see if a person has an enzyme present or absent due to a specific gene, and how the person handles a drug, how he or she metabolizes it, depends on this enzyme in some cases. Even so, this new criteria, which can help predict patient responses to an agent, is very limited. When someone swallows a pill, the doctor and the swallower are depending on current use and knowledge. The patient's body may respond unpredictably because his or her genetic construction and organ response is unique. Every pill swallowed is, therefore, an experiment.

Many patients believe a "natural" remedy is more applicable to their well-being than a chemical agent from a drug company's scientific study. This misplaced concept can do a great deal of harm. There is no natural agent that is superior because it's natural. A leaf from the ginkgo plant has chemicals just as dangerous as those of a pill. The idea of "natural" bamboozled many patients and caused them to avoid real help from the developed medicines.

The drugs used in psychiatry are faulty but useful, and they should be applied with caution and care in therapeutic situations. Unfortunately, they have been used for political reasons as well as therapeutic ones, and in these instances, they were harmful. For example, the old Soviet Union used Thorazine to subdue its dissidents. Families would visit their incarcerated loved ones and not recognize them because of their zombie-like appearance. These political prisoners were normal but were called schizophrenic by the hospital administrators under the aegis of the dictatorial government. Thorazine gave them the psychotic appearance the jailors needed to convince the Russian people that they were being protected. However, Thorazine was also one of the first effective drugs to quell psychotic aggression and excitement in patients who actually needed the drug. In this role, Thorazine was a godsend to suffering delusional patients who could not have a quiet, normal day of eating and sleeping. For these patients, treatment did not transform them into zombies but helped psychotic and hard-to-control human beings deal with the world more reasonably.

A simplistic view of psychiatric drugs has led many to refuse to understand their positive effects. The popular press fosters a huge debate regarding their efficacy. Some respectable writers have declared, for example, that antidepressants are not effective. Studies, using statistics, are often on the dubious edge of being convincing for these antiestablishment critics. They argue drugs are bad, and psychiatrists use them for monetary purposes not always for therapeutic.

In the practice of psychiatry, antidepressants seem very effective in a majority of cases, though not all. The tragedy that can come from untreated depression warrants that drugs be tried. Rather than allow a mother suffering from postpartum depression to kill her newborn in a delusional belief the child is a medium for the devil (to give one extreme example), the psychiatrist should use the antidepressants as an instrument of prevention.

Psychiatric drugs are not restoring chemical balance. Studies of neuronal receptors have shown many of these agents are working specifically on the neurons in the brain or their synapses, but it is not clear if this is the only place they are working. Receptor-site activity is an important part of drug efficacy, but the actual way in which this operates is complicated. The chemical messengers may be working in multiple areas in different ways. It leads to public expectations and misconceptions of what is in the troubled person. The receptors that are affected by the drugs are believed by the general public to simply being "balanced" chemically. This is not accurate and is overly simplistic. Affected, yes, balanced, no.

Drugs, then, are an important part of the clinician's care. As with any instrument, drugs can be misused or applied carefully in a considered manner. These chemicals can do good or cause harm. Agents such as these should never be elevated to a level of cure all, but neither should they be dismissed as merely harmful. Drugs are not the power-wielding hammer of the medical profession. They do not define what a doctor is. They are just another tool in the black medical bag and must be used judiciously.

PART 3

THE SENSIBLE LIFE

• • •

LIVING IS BASED ON A perceptual approximation in a sea of ambiguity. There is no certainty. The word *living* conjures up confidence, but there is no confidence in life. We approximate reality and consensually validate our findings with others. Uncertainty is predominant, vulnerability always inchoate. The certainty and confidence we feel is an illusion perpetrated by the culture our parents trained us to accept. Our daily feeling of comfort is a similarly imposed illusion, a marriage between the environment and our brains designed to give surety where there is mostly no surety. Within this miasma of vagueness about what reality is, we are living in a belief that the sun will rise the next day, and there will be no Cossack or Taliban invading our bedrooms. The nature of our existence is such that brain and environment seem, to whatever verifiability is possible, modestly accurate. Indeed the sun will shine tomorrow. The devil is in the details. Our visual perceptions are prone to error, and our behaviors are based on genetically given moods that affect our decision making. Our judgments come from years of cultural indoctrination, and the unconscious mind predominates while the consciousness we have acts as a check on whims and impulses. This is who we are.

To our amazement we feel none of this confusion and indeterminacy. Everything is in place via nature to give us the contrived feeling that all is well. Truly, it is better that way. Who could live each day fully tuned into all the uncertainties that beset us? It is better to pick and choose our ambiguities as they arise rather than dwell on their possibilities. This is what we do. However, reflection and consideration allow us to realize these potentially threatening aspects of reality and do what they can to forestall the consequences of ignorance. Highlighting the philosophical meaning of our existence does have value. It not only gives us the humility required to be reasonable people in a multivariable life, but also allows us to understand and prepare for the results of the ambiguities around us.

There is no sensible life. The sensible life in which we live is contrived from beliefs set in childhood and affected by knowledge and experience. Perhaps the *sense* of sensibility is the actual goal, some kind of concatenation of information and background that makes life seem as reasonable and consistent as possible. Since everything is an interpretation from the human perspective, we must try to interpret with humility and a keen awareness of its uncertainty. Life begins to make sense this way. This is the most we can hope for.

No one ever said living was easy or even sensible. It is neither. Like the concept of truth as an asymptote, living life becomes a struggle to approach satisfaction. The days of existence should be meaningful and enjoyable. Both the Stoicists and the Epicureans have been misinterpreted toward the extremes. The Stoicists did not believe all pleasure must be eliminated, and the Epicureans did not believe hedonism was the way to go. Both groups wanted to find a satisfying balance between pleasure and resigned satisfaction. For the Greeks (when they were able to think about these ideas rather than war upon each other), the extremes were to be avoided. Life was neither an indulgence nor a deprivation. Life was a gauntlet passed through, and one carefully avoided the beatings of too much of either a good thing or a punishment. Aristotle summed it up with *balance*: life was to be a balance among all extremes, searching for satisfaction while suffering the arrows of misfortune with as much fortitude and equanimity as possible.

Sadly, it is impossible to define *balance* comfortably. One could use the US Supreme Court's definition of *obscenity* determined in the famous case of James Joyce's novel, *Ulysses*. The justices had to decide whether or not to allow the new bawdy but trenchant fiction into the United States. The question before the Court was whether or not the book was obscene. One justice considered the question of just what obscenity was. His response is now famous: "I'll know it when I see it." This statement is hardly satisfying. The simple idea of avoiding extremes will have to do, while one person's extreme is often another person's balance. Language confounds us. However, sometimes the extreme does seem obvious.

This balance can be elusive, and each extreme can be somebody else's acceptable middle. For example, Michael Rockefeller was cannibalized because the New Guinea Asmat men who found him swimming near shore believed he needed to be eaten.[6] They felt the balance of their world could be sustained by eating a white man. Earlier, their tribesman had been killed by Dutch officials who were, of course, white. By killing and eating Michael, they regained the balance between suffering the losses of their friends and family and their ritual need to sustain their tribal beliefs.

Balance becomes a concept of culture. Within Western society, the idea has come to mean not emphasizing a behavior or thought to the point of dominance. You need to love, but do not love to the point of extinguishing yourself. You need to work, but you must not let work take over recreation and family. Money is important, but if it is the only end of a life's goal, money may lead to a great, maladaptive hurt. Consequently, you need enough money, but not so much as to cancel other values. How much do you need? That's a consideration everyone must decide. The balance comes from knowing yourself, your comfort zone, and what it takes to make your daily life work well for you. You must also have a future sense, predicting where your determined balance will lead you. Frustratingly, you read these words. Why can't he make this more specific? The answer is that there is no specific answer. The idea of balance is interpretable, as is everything else.

Someone working all night to make ends meet is clearly behaving to the extreme, and the result will be illness or simple exhaustion. Young doctors frequently run into this problem. Certainly, in medicine, it is possible to work twenty-four hours each day of the week. This absurdity requires that every doctor set a limit to his or her work schedule. Some

---

6 Carl Hoffman, "What Really Happened to Michael Rockefeller," in *Smithsonian*, March 2014.

do it well, and some do it poorly. The limit of work for every person is the balance between work, family, interests, and personal life.

There are those whose existence is neatly divided between family and work. These people have no other interests. They frequently dream of their children doing better: "I work for my children to have a better future." As admirable as this may seem, this is an unbalanced life. What's left out is the self. Whether it is friends, hobbies, or some special interest that pleases one a great deal, everyone is better pursuing something that excites him or her. This may be given the term "enlightened selfishness." Caring for the self and carving out a piece of time for the self from the family and marriage is nurturing. Those with a passionate calling as a sideline to family, work, and marriage are better for it. Though this is important throughout all the stages in life, it is especially significant during the older years and retirement. Having nothing to do can be as deleterious as being overworked.

This also provides a safety net for the marital relationship. Severe interdependency eats at the marriage. Each has to have a space for the self. Expecting the spouse to give meaning to life is a lost cause. Meaning is a combination of all the matters discussed, and no single person contributes to the question of what makes life valuable. Those forsaken widows who lived in their husbands' shadows and developed little individual fortitude or few interests find themselves like the Flying Dutchman, forever plying life's waters seeking meaning and love. Space becomes their *amour*, and empty space is never satisfying.

The sensible life depends, too, on how well the demons of childhood have been exorcised. Everyone has some issues that need attention and resolution. The overbearing father, the neglectful mother, the overindulgent mother, sibling rivalry, abuse, abandonment, and many other afflictions leave a scar on the adult. These injuries are sufferings that cannot be neglected. Their remnants eat away at any sense of well-being.

The narcissism of childhood distorts the true meaning of these difficult events; the child feels somehow responsible for his or her own situation. The planetoids of other people circle about the child, and the child feels him- or herself at the center. Whatever happens, the child believes, emanates from the central self.

This lingering sensitivity frequently continues to operate in the mind of the adult unless addressed and set to rest. Rarely are these adversities in any way caused by a child, yet adults often feel that they, as children, contributed to them. An adoptee feels her mother gave her away for adoption because she was not good enough; the adult often does not consider her mother had other issues that led to the adoption. Another child feels her mother neglectful because she, the child-now-adult, lacked some important quality. Considering the mother's situation at the time does not even factor in. A son is convinced his father was harsh because he was faulty, always making mistakes. He never considered the father was troubled and that the father too was abused similarly. Siblings fight because one thinks the other was more preferred by the parents.

None of these beliefs in adults stand up to the light of scrutiny, yet they plague many who think all these issues are behind them. No one can find the good life or the sensible life if these problems and con-flicts are not put in correct perspective. The correct perspective is that all events in life are complex combinations of personalities and events. Each contributes. The individual is merely part of the outcome, not the only cause, and probably not the most significant cause. All aspects of all circumstances, childhood or otherwise, have to be investigated and understood for there to be peace within the self.

The sensible life depends on good relationships. As discussed be-fore, these are the result of good, compatible choices. It is crucial to have an understanding of the elements in the self and the elements in the other person that create problems or disharmony. If a mate is so troubled as to make compromise impossible, the person suffering must consider breaking the relationship. Unreasonable expectations in others also cause problems. Very often a person hopes a marriage or love will settle or resolve childhood conflicts. While seeking desired help from a loved one, the residuals of childhood create difficulties in the relationship outside of awareness. To work out issues in a marriage, a full understanding of the self and the partner is essential.

A similar argument can be applied to one's children. Children are born to share life with the parents and are nurtured as part of the biological process. At no time are they to be a solution to parents' problems or parents' marriages. Their genetic endowment has to be respected. Some can do more than others; however, no child can or should be the answer to a parent's dream. The child develops for his or her sake, not for that of the parent. The great pleasure in rearing children is the reward of seeing them grow and enjoy life. Never should the child be treated as a solution to a parent's life problems.

From our discussion to this point, it is apparent that all of life becomes an interpretation. Nothing is easily categorized, and facts are never absolute. The arrangement of facts requires rules that are contrived by humans, and although some of the rules seem to fit nature, some do not. Rules give the semblance of certainty, but that is an illusion. Certainty is the never-obtained object of a lifelong quest. Rules and interpretations require language, and language is a uniquely human quality, emanating from the human brain and varying with culture and geography. Language is always metaphorical, always merely approximating truth.

If all of life is an interpretation, a mere approximation, how are we to manage? We manage with compromise, discussion, empathy, and the willingness to challenge confidence. If in the beginning there was the word, how do we live when we realize the word is a muddy ambiguity?

What do we do when we are aware words are open to anyone's interpretation, no matter how wildly inaccurate that meaning might prove to be? The word is human and only human. Other creatures have symbols and representations, but none have the language of poetry, multiple interpretations, and the uncertainties that we do.

We must recognize and confess to ourselves that we live only in an interpretable universe. We are merely part of a cosmological structure. This earth, this universe, is an idea we develop using words. The social structure, the rules that guide our daily interactions, is only implicitly meaningful, and the social order is an uncertain world when it comes to assessing status and individual worth. Our place in relationships and in groups is only the beginning of a sensible existence. We contrive our confidence from consensual validation determined by the culture in which we live. Overwhelming evidence to support our convictions is a requirement of daily living; we seek it as reassurance every time we get out of bed and enter the mainstream of the world in which we live.

The scientific method is not a dry, intellectual matter. It is not a belief system. No one should believe in science any more than he or she should believe in a doorknob. Science is a dynamic style of thinking in which all thoughts and meanings are tested. One hundred validations are not enough; one culture's validations are not enough. The confirmation of an idea is ongoing, inchoate, and never realized completely.

Fortunately, there are some interpreted certainties that we can usually take for granted. The presence of material objects is easily confirmed. Culture has rules that we can understand for the most part, even if the rules seem foolish at times. If a person stands in front of you with a loaded gun and shoots it at you, the bullet will hit you and do harm. If you cradle and comfort your child, he or she will probably respond with love for you. There are many probabilities in which we can feel confidence. There is little reason to challenge the obvious even though, often, the obvious is elusive. Most of daily life makes confirmable sense. Most of it fits the human rationale.

However, there are also many confusions because our brains are story makers. We do not always see what is there. Our eyes distort configurations. Hearing can falsely perceive what is not present and confuse what is transmitted as sound or verbal meaning. Our upbringing and our belief systems may configure the conclusions we derive. These conclusions based on childhood and adult learning may prove not commensurate with most people's conclusions. Social consensus may not be correct. We may not be correct. Understanding in life is more uncertain than people often admit. If we cross our arms, our right hands can misplace what our touch tells us, and we can locate the item in the wrong position. Any word or verbal idea can be interpreted in many ways. While we need our friends and family to confirm our thoughts on almost a moment-by-moment basis, we cannot accept their confirmations with certainty. Everything is an interpretation. Every communication requires testing, testing, testing.

How does anyone deal with this degree of uncertainty in everyday life? The first step, specified in this book, is to realize human limitations. Humans are a part of the biosphere. As far as the earth is concerned, humans are merely one earth ingredient among millions of others. The earth does not have a morality (though it may seem so from some biased and religious perspectives). All of its elements intertwine in a living menagerie of complex interaction. Religion, of course, turns this idea upside down, dictating that *Homo sapiens sapiens* is the most important earth element. The human is connected to God, and God is the administrator of the earth. "Man is made is God's image." However, perceptual and intellectual evidence leads us in another direction.

Once we consider humanity as the most important part of the earth because of its connection to a God, then the contradictions start coming.

Effecting the annihilation of millions of people in the thirteenth and fourteenth centuries, the Black Plague defies this conclusion. Voltaire saw the Lisbon earthquake of the seventeenth century as the defining factor in his disbelief in God the planner. The morality of God comes into question over and over. Religion protects its beliefs with the strange platitude that "God works in mysterious ways." As devastation upon devastation occurs to Candide, Voltaire has Dr. Pangloss say, "This is still the best of all possible worlds." The sarcasm drips off the sentence.

If the idea of God creates contradictions once human beings are seen as the center of the earth's purpose, what does the opposite view hold? The godless view is that humans are part of the earth and are not chosen by a deity to be special. If humans are special, their specialness is a remarkable aspect of nature that remains a mystery. There is no morality in the fact of human existence. Humans, as animals of the biosphere, are neither good nor bad. They simply are. If humans want to make themselves special, superior, and more important than all other living things, there is nothing to stop them. This is a result of their bias and not the result of some intervening deity.

This conclusion for many provokes powerful anxiety. The idea that there is nowhere to turn on this planet except toward the sensibility of the human population itself is a sobering one. If there is no father figure in the sky or elsewhere to pray to, and no amount of prayer will result in a kind of celestial parental rescue, humankind is left to its own resources. Whether the genus survives or not depends partly on itself and partly on the variegations of the planet on which it depends. Humans are clever, remarkably so, and it is up to them to use this intelligence to sustain themselves. This is not a secular view as much as a view based on what can be learned from the world in which we live. Dispel the facts, and you need God. Keep the facts, and you may need God but be hesitant to have a faith that leads to contradictions, failed hopes, unanswered prayers, and confused logic.

Another side of this existential dilemma is that humankind must turn to humankind to solve the problem of living. The power of the sapient brain is enormous, and people, as a cooperative group, might be able to lengthen life, increase health, improve technology, assist the environment in making the world healthier, and provide a biosphere that enhances life. The "we're all in the same boat" philosophy may be helpful. Rather than waging religious wars over who is closer to the true God, we can consider the best cooperative effort to improve life. Aggression and destruction becomes counterproductive. Balance and cooperation becomes productive and enhancing.

Human issues often seem to be a result of the need to resolve which sibling or which culture is the best. This guarantees strife. If survival and the good life can be available to all, then the issue dissolves. It no longer matters which sister is best or which society is superior. The issue then becomes making people and all cultures as good as possible. Differences become differences and no more. There is no productive good in trying to prove one person or culture better than the other. Just because you kill your enemy doesn't mean much in the way of your personal value. It doesn't mean you're better or stronger; it only means you've killed your enemy. If you get pleasure from this success, you are only creating the self-imposed delusion that might makes right. The dead cannot acknowledge their defeat. You become, like most deluded kings of history, the fool who thinks dominance is the only important value in life.

If any of this sounds utopian or paradisiacal, it is not meant to be. There is no paradise, and there never was one. Adam and Eve in the garden of Eden are a metaphor to deaden the pain of daily living and death, as all myths are. Earth itself is the only concern that warrants the utopian vision. Earth is the utopia of air, water, life that's sustainable. This precious orb requires care and attention to its maintenance. We can ignore its needs or feel the responsibility of keeping it nutritive for humanity. Earth is a complex arrangement of interacting molecules of an undetermined future. If anything, earth is a human-marred nonutopia that needs care. If it's to be any kind of genuine utopia, humanity must do its job to make it so.

If humans want to continue living on the planet, they have to cooperate in making home healthy, clean, and livable. There are always problems. There will probably always be mysteries. The universe, the solar system, the planet, and life on the planet have not released their enigma solutions yet. We must learn all we can about what we have. Utopia is not a practical vision. The Earth is. Earth is where we must place our best effort.

• • •

A DAY IN A SENSIBLE LIFE

Upon awakening every morning, we have to decide to live. This is what the existentialist philosophers argue, and it seems to be a worthwhile idea. Entering into the day with a conscious obligation to ourselves to fill it with meaningful experiences is a responsibility not left to idle consideration. By feeling this commitment, we are sharing the planet's persistence with a will of our own. Life becomes not a passive participation in a world already before us but an active decision to take part in personal and planetary activities. With this in mind, we acknowledge ourselves as part of the biosphere, an element, a self, in a world we want to perpetuate. By this early act of the day, our presence is no mere add-on to the earth's rotation. Our lives become an assertion.

To be able to make this conscious decision on a daily basis, we have to be secure within ourselves. We need the knowledge, the health, and the economic essentials to sustain such a philosophy.

As we brush our teeth, comb our hair, put on our makeup, and finish our toilet, we consider the day. We should be anticipating a one filled with meaningful activities. Work is an essential element, and it should be the kind of work we enjoy. If circumstance results in work being a tolerated endeavor to earn the essential money for our well-being and our family's comfort, we must see this as a compromise from the ideal. In these cases, we must make all efforts to change this unpleasant work situation, but often it cannot be changed. Our inner peace depends on a realistic appraisal of the workday and its necessity. If we must endure the unpleasant, the unpleasant should be a sequestered sensibility placed aside the more emotionally important matters in life.

If work includes caring for children, then the day is a busy and pre-occupying one. Children demand constant and intense attention. This is not a secondary occupation, downgraded from going into the out-of-home workforce to earn a salary. Childcare is a primary job; it is demanding and sometimes exhausting, and a requirement for children who later want to lead sensible lives. The end of the working day for a person involved in childcare should be based on the best job done, not the overt thankful appreciation of the children. Children absorb childcare like a sponge and have no awareness of the work involved. The engrossed concern for the welfare of children during the day has to be its own reward. Their happiness and continued health is primary to the overall job. Waiting for the child to express his or her appreciation is waiting for Godot; it just doesn't happen.

Living sensibly cannot be done alone, and relationships are crucial as a support system. Conflict always arises in families, and matters must be settled so that every relation feels respected and cared for. Issues of anger and discontent must be resolved, for no one can enter onto a new day with family irritations on the mind. The more comfortable the family relationships, the easier the day, even with a bad job, will seem.

As the day progresses, you will have many encounters. Those you meet will have problems and will deal with you accordingly. You will realize this psychological separation between you and other people and will discount irritations resulting from these problems. No one represents accurately who you are; your sense of worth does not depend on what he or she says or does not say. Disappointments are managed by a realization that your narcissism plays no role in the relationship, except to alert you to injury. You have no need to show others your worth, and you can feel comfort that their worth is their responsibility. In this regard, thoughtful and empathic attitudes are the important ones and should be conveyed. Your responsibility is not to help others to live better unless they ask. You are limited in what you can do, and you accept this limitation as a part of your life.

For the most part, you will pay your bills on time. You appreciate contracts when you owe for services rendered, and payment should be prompt. However, you realize the world is unpredictable and often others will try to take advantage. You will defend your position when this happens without attacking the other person. Anger is kept to a minimum. Anger has effects on the body, and you should allow this emotion only when it serves a purpose. This ideal can rarely be maintained, but it is an ideal to be approached.

Communications with others are thoughtful and considerate. Sarcasm is a veiled attack and should rarely be used. However, humor and double entendre are part of the language fabric; these artifices can be helpful in controversial exchanges. Wit is a healthy outlet as long as it does not reach the level of hurtful sarcasm. It is always important to read the receptivity of the object of your wit or humor so that unmeant hurts can be corrected instantly.

Most days are somewhat stressful. When you return home, you remain aware that your spouse, lover, or roommate has had a day similar to yours. Venting to each other is healthy and desirable. Couples who don't share their difficulties do not have promising futures. Listening carefully, asking questions, and offering suggestions are the important aspects of this sharing.

You remain aware of your body, its functions, and its fatigue. Sleep is essential, and you are careful to give yourself enough. Sexual activity is part of any relationship. The day may end with sexual pleasure or simply with relaxed sharing. Always show appreciation for what others do for you. Never take this for granted. Problems that arise for each during the day must be shared and resolved as much as possible.

As you consider sleep, your perspective on the year is in your mind. There are things you wish to do, places you wish to see, and these should always be used as a kind of future salve for any aggravations of the day. Special interests are important. Never trivialize interests of others because everything about both of you deserves your regard. Share with your partner any plans for the weekend when matters are more relaxed. Touching at this time is important and makes a relaxed presleep state more likely to attenuate insomnia. If possible, avoid issues that provoke agitation or conflict during this presleep period. They should be addressed before going to bed, discussed and resolved. If there were any ongoing stresses in the day, measures must be taken to settle them at a more appropriate hour to reduce their effect on sleep.

Despite childcare and other issues, couples should go to bed at the same time. Sleep onset should be close for each. Sharing and lights out are the mainstays of this period. Brief pillow talk is desirable.

The day starts with each other and ends with each other.

A Dialogue between Patrick and RDM

Patrick: I've enjoyed your book. I think it's a bit pompous and sometimes outright wrong, but it has made me think, and this is something I don't like to do very much. Life is too short. I try not to worry about love, death, and other people too much. I'd rather just have fun. In a way I'm glad you made me read your ideas, but in another way I'd just rather go to sleep.

RDM: So why bother even talking with me? Why did you call me to have lunch? I was surprised, especially when you agreed to pay.

P: I have the money, and I know you don't. We've always been friends. I mean, I kind of liked you in high school. You were the nerd, but you were always friendly to me. When I saw you wrote this book and you lived in New York only twenty minutes from me, I decided to read *The Sensible Life* and to call you for lunch. All of that's not so weird, is it?

RDM: No, not at all. I was delighted to hear from you and saw lunch as a wonderful opportunity to see you and find out what you thought about my book. I looked forward to this meeting. I've never been in the Grill Room of the Four Seasons restaurant. I read it's the power room where many powerful men have lunch. I want to thank you in advance for this opportunity.

P: Well, you're welcome in advance. The way I see it, your book is in two big sections. The first is a lot of psychology. [In] the second part, you move into philosophy. I know you're a psychiatrist, but I wondered what right you had to espouse philosophy.

RDM: I have no right at all. I have none of the credentials of an academic philosopher. I can think and reflect. I can base my conclusions partly on what I've read, but I have no legitimate claim to being a philosopher. Perhaps it was a bit of hubris for me to write down my philosophical thoughts. I felt compelled to open a dialogue regarding how I saw things. From reading, I got the idea my views were not popular nor extant, so I decided to put them in writing to share them with others.

It was a selfish act of pleasure. As I see it, I'm part of the world in which other thinking people live, and [I] want others to consider my ideas. Always I hope to learn something from the endeavor.

P: Then I guess you won't mind being challenged?

RDM: It would be a great pleasure to me.

P: I don't want to seem insulting or harsh, but I think most of what you said is a lot of crap.

RDM: [He laughs] I can handle it. Don't hold back.

P: You know, of course, that Freud has been discredited as an opinionated philosopher rambling on in many books with no scientific facts?

RDM: This is now a popular idea about Freud. Of course I know that.

P: And you are doing the same?

RDM: Yeah, I guess so. I give a lot of credit to Freud despite this widely held view and feel honored to be in his shadow.

P: I thought your emphasis on sibling rivalry was important, but it's just your opinion. I'm not sure the world will agree that it's the basis for tyrants and despots.

RDM: Like any idea of merit, it has its limits. I think it often plays a role in power grabs and is underappreciated.

P: There are no real facts to back it up.

RDM: That's the main point. There are no real facts at all. There are only interpretations.

P: There you go. There are no real facts? Two plus two isn't four?

RDM: It seems to be true, but it's based on our view of numbers defined by language.

P: Again. Everything is language.

RDM: Can't escape it. Even "two" is a language concept. At the simplest level, it's two fingers, two units added, two items; but it gets weird when you take its square root or try to reconcile its log base. I admit that at its simplest two is two, but its meaning becomes elaborated as you dig into the way it's used.

P: Oh, man, you do go on.

RDM: Yeah, I've got to watch myself. Sorry. But all meanings, even something as simple as the number two, is hidden, and our only means to deal with [them] is language. I've always been impressed how much this is ignored by trained philosophers (those I've read, anyway.)

P: OK, if everything is language, what's the big deal? It's a word, and we can understand words.

[The waiter comes by, pours water, and asks if they would like to order. They do. Patrick gets the New York strip steak. RDM gets a salad frisée with chicken. The waiter leaves.]

RDM: Words come from our brains. Words are communication constructs depending on neuronal concordance. We don't even know how the brain['s] neuronal networks translate thoughts into words. It's amazing really.

P: Whoa! You're getting big words on me. Stop. How am I supposed to follow this technical jargon? Keep it simple.

RDM: Sorry. I really didn't mean to get stuffy and sound arrogant, but basically, words are like colors or sounds. They come from our brains. We can hear and see only a small part of sounds available and colors around us. We interpret what we can without even knowing we're estimating meaning. Words work the same way, but we usually aren't aware of their limitations. Day-to-day experiences are easily managed without concern about ambiguity or confusions. It's when we get into explaining difficult ideas like reality and meaning that words show their limitations. My concern is only that this is too often ignored.

P: So you've got the same problem with words as the rest of us, right? What you're saying right now remains partly uncertain because of word limitations?

RDM: I think that's right, yet words are all we have. All I want is for everyone to acknowledge their limitations.

P: So how do we know anything for sure, especially if all words have a built-in uncertainty?

RDM: We don't. Life is a blur with islands of meaning we accept because we're all in the same boat.

P: You mean there is no external reality? The world is vague?

RDM: We assume we live in a world of external reality, but our understanding of it is limited by our senses. Our senses are our unique biologies giving us a confident idea of the world in which we live. This sensual reality is our own. A bee, an ant, a chimp, an oryx—if they could talk—might see our world differently. Language is another sense that puts an additional barrier to understanding while it enhances our social skills. In ordinary life, this is no impediment. It becomes a problem when we become philosophical or scientific and dig deep into the foundations of what the external world is.

P: So from your point of view there is a real world beyond us.

RDM: Yes. Plato's cave is an example of sensory illusion, but Plato did not appreciate the fact that the unbound cave dwellers seeing beyond the shadows of the cave had to use language to describe the world they experienced. He never appreciated that language was just as much a shadow as those the fires were making. This is also why his search for arête, virtue, always seemed wanting.

P: [How] can we know anything, by your way of thinking?

RDM: We can't. Knowledge and truth are always the Holy Grail out of reach, but we get close enough to live comfortably. Remember my little adage: truth is an asymptote, and everything we sense requires an interpretation.

P: Taking this to its ultimate, you would say that life is an ambiguous human experience couched in a vocabulary that is merely an estimate of what is in the world.

RDM: Exactly.

P: So the sensible life is the sensually limited life?

RDM: Yes. Thank you for understanding me so well.

P: So what is reality beyond our senses? How do we know it?

RDM: We don't. We estimate it. We use science with a capital *S*. This means we don't trust ourselves. We gather information, we test the information, and we look for inconsistencies in the information we believe in.

P: Confidence is an illusion?

RDM: Yes, it's an illusion [that] we need to function in our ordinary day. I certainly would not want to scientifically check every one of my perceptions and convictions all the time. It's only when we espouse values, look for explanations, and try to explain the world that we have to be humble, careful, and scientific.

P: How do we know when our values are right? Good, bad, right, wrong—do none of these have any objective basis?

RDM: No. None. They are language bound in our various cultures. There is no celestial guide to establish these values for all of us. Only humans make values. This is so terribly uncertain that early mankind created deities to send down these values. By attributing good and bad to a god or gods, societies gave weight to the rules most of its members agreed upon. There is no absolute good that all cultures adhere to.

P: No one wants to die. That's a good rule. Don't kill.

RDM: It's a good rule for us. It does not apply to the wildebeest being chased by the lioness. There is no rule for the animal feeling, "Don't kill me." This rule is for humans only.

P (smiling): In the beginning there was the word, and the word was human, right? Not God?

RDM: I'm afraid so. God was invented by humans to give power to their rules, rules created by them for themselves. This is why his existence creates so many confusions. "Why did they all die in the Lisbon earthquake? Why must we suffer so when we have been virtuous?" The answers are not couched in the priest's reply that "God works in mysterious ways." The answer is inherent in the context that we are of this world and shit happens.

P: We live then with rules of our own making. The better the rules, the more humans thrive. The worse the rules, the more likely the human race will perish on, as Shakespeare would say, their own "petard."

RDM: This is my view. The good news is that daily life can be rewarding and enjoyable. The Western world has caught on to the necessity for humans [to make] rules and standards of life that help humans thrive. This can be improved upon. Bentham tried to create a consistent philosophy to back up the human system.

P: I know. That which is best for all. The greater good.

RDM: It's simply impossible to know this. Most benefit from a good water supply, but for some that means their land must be confiscated. Each moral problem must be decided on its own merits. A rule to cover all moral quandaries is impossible. The idea that humans should have rules that are best for humans is a good rule if you're human. For us, it is the only reasonable morality, but it is by its nature selfish, or, if you prefer, humanish.

P: How do you know if a person is good or bad, right or wrong, superior or inferior, if all values are ambiguous?

RDM: All values are arbitrary. They are based on human determinations. They are cultural. I think humans are better for recognizing this.

P: You must admit that the crimes of ISIS, abusing and subjugating women, beheading innocent people, burning pilots alive, and mass executions are wrong?

RDM: To me, yes, they are wrong. To ISIS they are not. The culture of ISIS gives a "good" to these acts. The larger culture of humanity sees that humanity is threatened if the ISIS view is sustained. From the view of the greater culture, the mass of humanity, this kind of horrific behavior cannot be allowed or all will perish in its consequences.

P: So we can say ISIS is wrong. We can say it's not practical. We can say that there is a larger morality than the parochial ISIS brand?

RDM: I agree with all of that except I add the proviso that you are arguing one facet of humanity's values (albeit the largest in number) over a smaller facet.

P: Really, must we pander to this liberal cultural relativism?

RDM: It's not cultural relativism. There is no wish to say ISIS's value is right in its context and the greater good is right in its context. Right and wrong are not relative: they are just human determinants. If I believe ISIS must be contained and [its] behavior prevented, it's because I determine that humanity is probably best served by limiting religious intolerance and terror. This is a determination, not an absolute truth. We humans try to form a moral code to fit a predetermined good outcome. There is nothing absolute about it. There is deific origin. We can create a deific origin, as in the Ten Commandments, but this is a contrivance to obtain power or conviction over doubt, not a true edict from a grand and lordly source. The latter is a human illusion.

P: If everything is language, and language is human, then are you saying all values are human, none derive from nature?

RDM: If you look at nature dispassionately, you see animals killing animals for food without discretion or morality. Storms come and go independent of the goodness or badness of the trees and animals they destroy. Earthquakes level buildings and kill wantonly. A gazelle is captured and eaten by the lioness not because it's a bad gazelle, but because it is slower. We humans add the morality and talk scientifically of the evolutionary benefit of culling a herd or balancing the ecology. These are merely human concerns. We, rather, live on a planet with characteristics we struggle to understand. Nature is amoral. Whatever reason it has is given by us for us.

P: If we follow your views, there are no values. We attract nihilism and chaos. Yours is a philosophy of despair with no religion to give morality.

RDM: The truth is better than the fiction with which we've lived our lives this past one hundred thousand years. We are merely part of this planet's ecology, no more. With our remarkable brains using our sensory systems couched in language, we have an advantage over other fauna, and we should use this advantage. We often do appreciate the thinking required to enable the best way to exist on the planet; rather, we live in fearful ignorance. In our anxiety we have invented deities to back up prejudices and standards. These moralities have led to misery for millions of us. The old human adage of "working together" is the only value system that makes sense. All of us are among all the animals on this planet. Some have skills others don't have, and these skills must be appreciated. This doesn't mean the person with the skill is superior, only possessed of the skill. The superior-inferior evaluation derives from the survival necessity of one sibling over another. Sibling rivalry does a great deal to set up this morality. We must realize the basis for our beliefs and mold a society based on our wish to survive and thrive.

P: So religion is out.

RDM: Religion as a core value based on mythic tales of celestial beings influencing humans on this planet is out.

P: Democracy is inefficient, argumentative, and, looking at the example of the deaths of Socrates, Lavosier, and others, is hurtful.

RDM: Humans are animals, an imperfect species, severely prone to error. However, we must govern ourselves with some underlying philosophy. The greatest good for the greatest number doesn't work because the minority or the singular is often a victim. Survival of the fittest doesn't work because it really applies to an unvalued system of species continuation based on natural occurrences. It cannot be applied, Ayn Rand–style, to aggressive beings passionate to be despots. Democracy is sloppy, prone to human folly, [and] sometimes terribly wrong, but its principle of trying to determine, through popular consensus, the most beneficial laws for all is probably the best we can contrive at the moment. Lately [2015], I have been troubled by the US Congress showing a lack of concern for reasonable governance, but I would not dissolve the process. We must restore the sense of mission. The mission is to govern for all and not for selfish interests. Overall, I think the spirit of United States is on the right track; I only worry that it might lose its way to the extent [that] we might have anarchy.

P: Your philosophy leaves me very nervous.

RDM: Me, too. I often wish there was a proper god that we, in good child-to-parent style, could rely upon. That would be a fool's dream.

P: If everything is a perceptual uncertainty, if all understanding is based on interpretation, if language is our trap (I recently learned there are over seven thousand languages), if there are hundreds of human ways of living and multiple cultures using different combinations, how does a thinking person comfortably exist? What makes us comfortable every day if everything is uncertain?

RDM: You do get to the heart of the matter. Living without religion does not produce an easy philosophy. Once you realize that language and you are the arbitrary inventions of our biosphere, you can easily give up in a quandary of uncertainty. If there is a solution, it has to do with adaptation to the context in which you were born. This doesn't mean you have to believe in all the values and philosophies of your context, or Western civilization for that matter; it means you have to realize it's all contrived by humans evolving over time. There are many directions, values, and philosophies that can develop. You happen to be in one of them. You have no choice but to live within the context given. If you want nonconformist thoughts or ideas, that is fine. Just realize that you are creating your own context, and it may be alien to others. It's very difficult to see the world as a palimpsest, an extant tablet on which cultures write their melodies, but that's what it is. Context is everything. We manage it through interpretation and adaptation. Our brains are coincident with context. The danger is trying to find universal ideas or values, struggling to say this moral thesis is perfect and that one is wrong. A utilitarian view helps sometimes, but not all the time. The greater number does not always deserve the spoils, just as the small minority does not always deserve the remains. Arguing universals is a fruitless enterprise. Understanding context and adapting to it begins in childhood. This makes it easier. Only when absolutes are pursued does the meaning of context really show its power. Is there an ideal for the world? Depends on the context and values. Should human values be the rule of law? Depends on whether you're an orangutan. Finding the context, understanding the context, and adapting to context make it possible to live.

P: So we are all sensualists, depending on our senses and languages to interpret the world in order to make the best of it. Would you say that's the "sensible life?" Did you mean to give your title that double meaning? "Sensible" meaning reasonable and open-eyed, and "sense-able" meaning understanding the limits and necessity of our senses?

RDM: You know, Patrick, you have always understood me so well. I'm so happy to have you as my friend.

P: Thanks. I feel the same.

RDM: Oh, and thanks for lunch, too. It was great.

P: You are very welcome…in this context.

AUTHOR BIOGRAPHY

• • •

ROBERT D. MARTIN, MD, HAS been a practicing clinical psychiatrist for nearly fifty years. With a lifetime of experience behind him, he is still dedicated to trying to help people in any way he can.

Dr. Martin's debut book, *The Sensible Life*, takes a philosophical look at how individuals interpret the experience of life. He is currently working on his first novel.